MY FATHER, THE MAN WHO NEVER WAS

Ronnie Reed:
The Life and Times of an MI5 Officer
in his own words

Expanded and illustrated
by his son Nicholas Reed

Best Wishes,
Nicholas Reed
October 2012

Lilburne Press

This First Impression of the First Edition is limited to 1000 copies

Published by Lilburne Press
7 Wingate Road, Folkestone, Kent CT19 5QE
Telephone: 01303 257 659

www.lilburnepress.co.uk

ISBN 978-1-901167-21-4

Printed by Buckland Media Group Ltd
Dover, Kent CT17 0LG

Also by Nicholas Reed:

Sisley on the Thames and the Welsh Coast
Pissarro in West London
Frost Fairs on the Frozen Thames
Folkestone – Then and Now

Ronnie Reed at about the age of 12.

Ronnie Reed: An Introduction

IN DECEMBER 1994, my father knew he did not have long to live. He had inoperable cancer, and would probably be dead within a few months. (In fact, he died on 24th January 1995.) I had given up trying to persuade him to let me interview him about his top secret work. He refused to discuss it, though he sometimes let slip the odd anecdote. However, I thought it might be nice if there was a filmed interview with someone who ran double-agents, including Agent Zigzag, during the War, and had been in MI5 from the 1940s until his retirement. So he agreed to let me film him talking about innocuous matters, just as a film record of an interesting man.

Having agreed the interview with him a week in advance, I rang up the day before, when he seemed to have changed his mind. "What is the point of an interview?" he said. "You can see what people look like from photographs." I replied that photos give no idea of someone's personality, that I had tape-recorded his mother reminiscing, and that, with modern technology, it would be even better to watch him in a video interview, and get a much better idea of his personality. He reluctantly agreed.

When we met the following day, he asked at the start what we were going to talk about. I said, "Perhaps we could talk about St Christopher's Hospice, which you visited recently." He replied, "Well, I could do that if you like. But if you prefer, I could tell you how I got involved in The Office during the War, and then take it from there." I was delighted that, at last, he was willing to talk, and started the interview. It seems my father had thought hard about it, and decided there was nothing wrong in putting on record what he had done, especially now he would no longer be around to face the consequences of "breaking the Official Secrets Act". Watching the interview now, I think in fact he became slightly impatient to get on to talk about his secret work, when I was asking him questions about the BBC in the early days.

Agent Zigzag

He described, very coherently, much of what he had done. He omitted one point. This was in talking about the agent Eddie Chapman. In the recorded interview, he failed to mention his own flight out to Lisbon to see Chapman, and a week later, when he was not well enough for me to record an interview with him again, he told me he was kicking himself for having omitted that episode. He then described it in detail to me, and I wrote it straight down afterwards.

Operation Mincemeat

In printing the interview and setting it in context, I have tried to keep to chronological order, but with one exception. Last year saw the publication of two books retelling the remarkable story of *The Man Who Never Was.* Since the title of this book claims that my father was The Man, I need to start by explaining this, and perhaps thereby kindle the reader's interest in a man of very humble origins who ended up taking an important role in the deception programme which finally enabled us to win the Second World War.

Nicholas Reed
Folkestone 2011

CONTENTS

ILLUSTRATIONS

Unless otherwise stated, photos reproduced are taken by the author, or from the author's collection. In some cases, they come from Wikipedia Commons.

Every reasonable effort has been made to trace copyright holders of material reproduced in this book, but if any have been inadvertently overlooked, the publishers would be glad to hear from them.

All photos on pages 19-21 were supplied by The Citadel Archives and Museum, Charleston, South Carolina

ONE

RONNIE REED AND OPERATION MINCEMEAT

ONE OF the most famous of the deception plans in which my father was involved, is sometimes known as *The Man who Never Was*. It took place in 1943, and its code-name at the time was Operation Mincemeat.

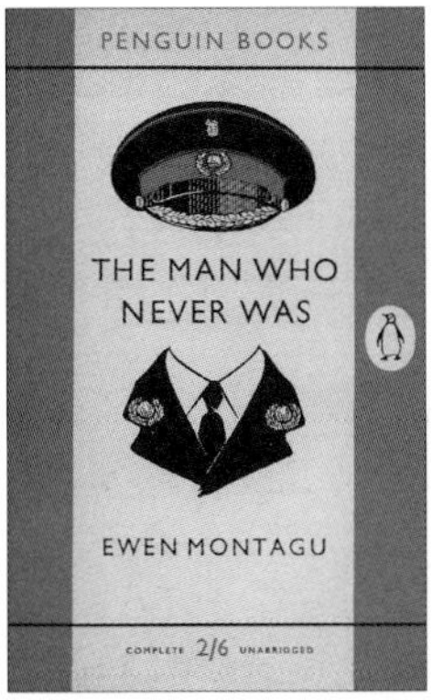

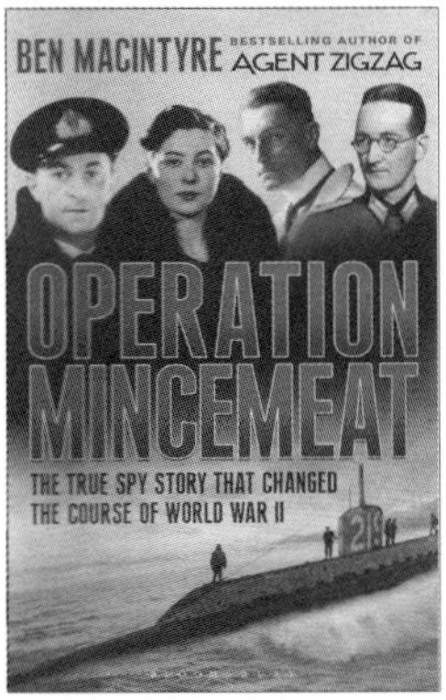

Right: the first Penguin edition of *The Man Who Never Was*, published in 1956. *Centre:* the latest reprint, published by OUP in 1996. *Far right: Operation Mincemeat*, published by Bloomsbury.

The carrying out of this deception plan was described in the book *The Man who Never Was*, by Ewen Montagu, published in 1953, and in the film with the same name, starring Clifton Webb and Maurice Denham, which was launched in 1956. For the fullest account of the whole operation, see now *Operation Mincemeat* by Ben Macintyre (2010).

By 1943, the balance of power had shifted in the Mediterranean. The Allies had forced Rommel out of Africa, and the next logical step would be to launch an invasion on some part of the Mediterranean coast north of Africa, on or before the invasion of France. But to do so, Sicily would have to be their first target: its position in the middle of the Mediterranean made it an obvious stepping stone to reach the Italian mainland. In any case, if they had left Sicily in German hands, it would be impossible for our invasion forces to capture and supply their targets further north: bombing raids from the Germans in Sicily would have slaughtered our troops landing in almost any coastal beach on the Med. So our first target really had to be Sicily. But this was not so obvious to the Germans, who really did not know where the attack on the "soft underbelly of Europe" would come.

Montagu suggested the Allies should try to place a body in German hands, containing what seemed to be highly secret documents containing details of the proposed invasion plans for the Mediterranean. These would indicate that Sardinia and Greece were the principal targets. Montagu attributed the idea to a friend of his whom he gave the code-name George. George's real name has since been revealed as that of Flight Lieutenant Charles Cholmondeley.

In order for the Germans to "find" these plans, they should seem to have been accidentally lost. Montagu therefore suggested they should get hold of a body, invent an identity for it, plant the "secret" plans on it, and then land it on the coast of Spain. Though Spain was officially neutral during the War, Franco's fascist leadership meant his officials were very sympathetic to the Nazis, and one could almost guarantee the Spaniards would allow the Germans to see these "confidential" documents. If the body was left at sea just off the coast of Spain, it would look as though his plane had come down and his body had been washed ashore.

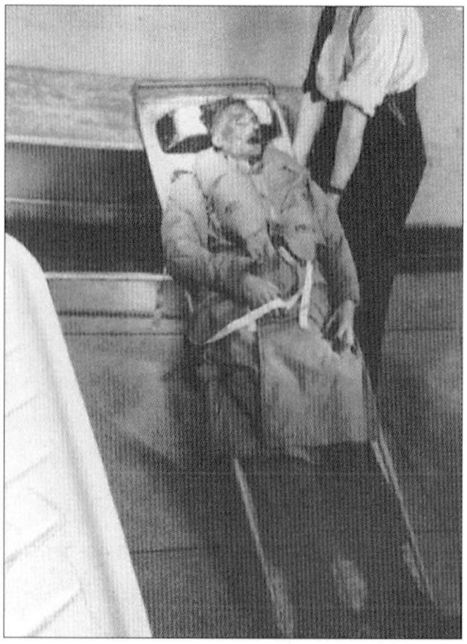

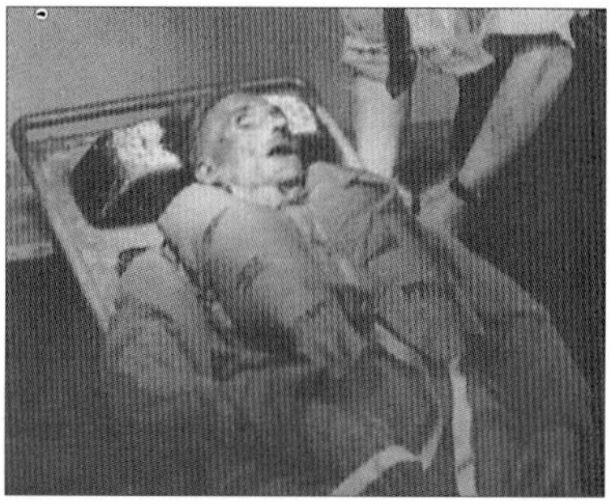

The body of Glyndwr Michael, dressed as Major William Martin, in the mortuary at Hackney.

Montagu was able to obtain the body of a tramp, who had died of phosphorus poisoning. If traces of liquid were found in the lungs, this was likely to be diagnosed as seawater from his supposed drowning, rather than the poisoning which created it.

They next had to create an identity for the body, so the Germans could believe he might well have been carrying important plans. Hence the creation of "Major William Martin".

The most striking way in which my father was involved in the whole project was during the making of the identity card for Major Martin.

To do this, they needed a photo of "the Major". They first tried taking a photo of the corpse, but, as Montagu said, "It is impossible to describe how utterly and hopelessly dead any photograph of the body looked". Eventually, he decided to use a photo which would do. After all, few people resemble their photos very closely, and one could hope the Germans would feel the same.

The Identity Card of "Major Martin"

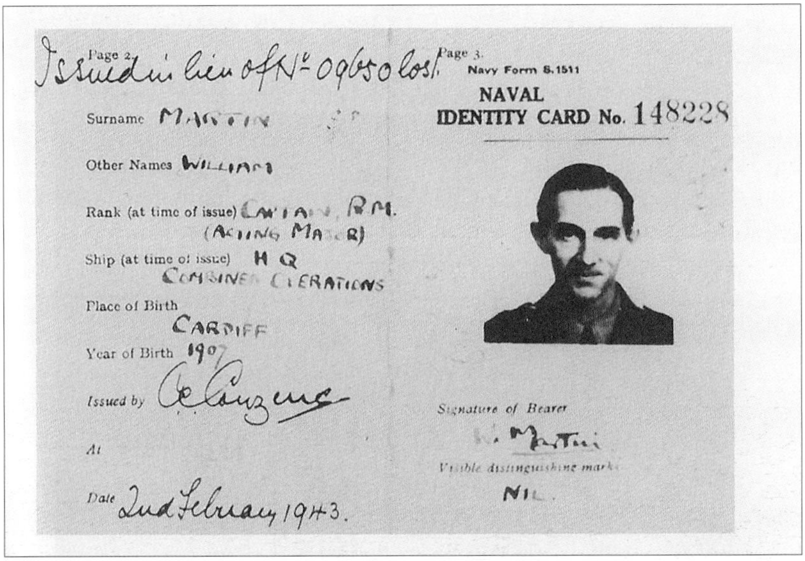
Issued in lieu of No 09650 lost.

Page 2. Page 3.

Navy Form S.1511

NAVAL IDENTITY CARD No. 148228

Surname MARTIN

Other Names WILLIAM

Rank (at time of issue) CAPTAIN, R.M. (ACTING MAJOR)

Ship (at time of issue) H Q COMBINED OPERATIONS

Place of Birth CARDIFF

Year of Birth 1907

Issued by

At

Date 2nd February 1943.

Signature of Bearer W. Martin

Visible distinguishing marks NIL.

The Identity Card of Ronnie Reed, when he was in New Zealand in 1959

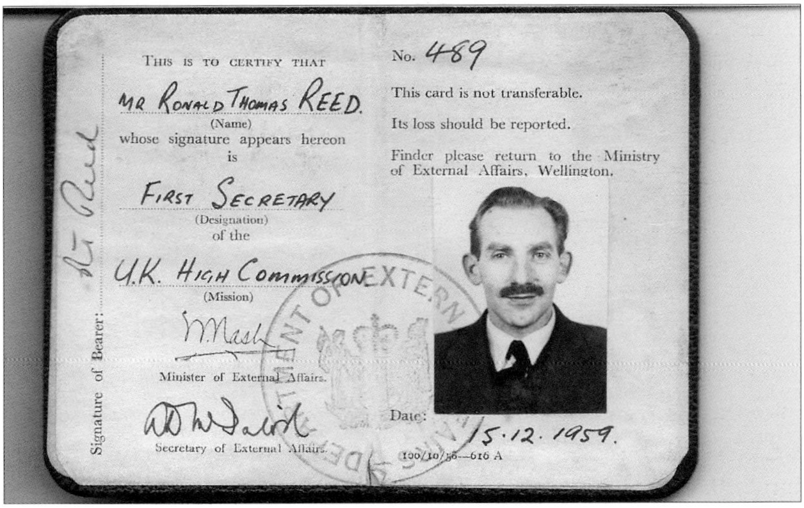
THIS IS TO CERTIFY THAT

MR RONALD THOMAS REED
(Name)
whose signature appears hereon is

FIRST SECRETARY
(Designation)
of the

U.K. HIGH COMMISSION
(Mission)

Minister of External Affairs.

Secretary of External Affairs.

Signature of Bearer: R T Reed

No. 489

This card is not transferable.

Its loss should be reported.

Finder please return to the Ministry of External Affairs, Wellington.

Date: 15.12.1959.

100/10/56—616 A

And then, wrote Montagu, "Sitting opposite to me at a meeting to deal with quite a different matter, I saw someone who might have been the twin brother of the corpse." Under a pretext, he asked him if he could please have a photograph, which would be used for an official purpose. My father agreed, which is why the passport photo of *The Man Who Never Was*, is in fact a photograph of my father!

The meeting was to discuss the case of Agent Zigzag, so, as his Case Officer, my father would have been there. But we also know that Ronnie must have been let into the secrets of Mincemeat, because in the photo taken for the Identity Card of Major Martin, he is dressed in a marine's uniform, which the Major would have worn, if he had existed.

My mother once explained that when my father first dressed up for work at The Office, he looked far too young for the job. They decided he would grow a moustache to look a little bit older! He kept the moustache until the 1970s. I show a photo from 1959, with a moustache, in which you can see he still has a great resemblance to the photo used in the fake Identity Card. The same prominent nose and rather large ears are visible in both photos.

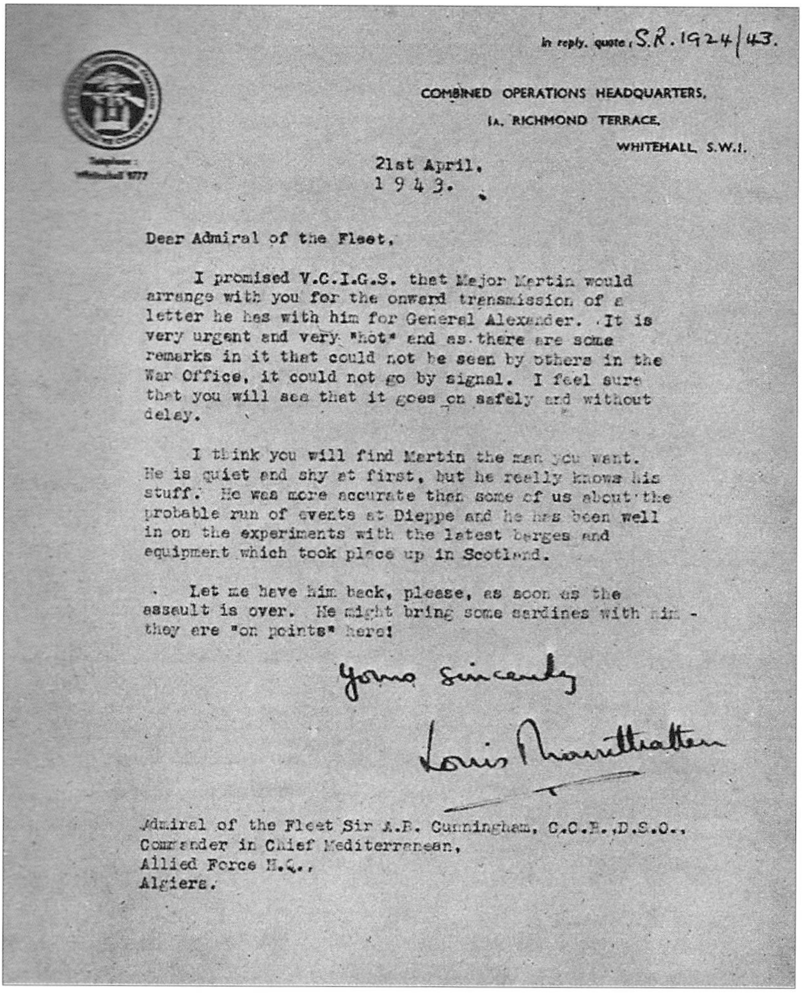

In reply, quote: S.R. 1924/43.

COMBINED OPERATIONS HEADQUARTERS,
1A, RICHMOND TERRACE,
WHITEHALL, S.W.1.

21st April,
1943.

Dear Admiral of the Fleet,

I promised V.C.I.G.S. that Major Martin would arrange with you for the onward transmission of a letter he has with him for General Alexander. It is very urgent and very "hot" and as there are some remarks in it that could not be seen by others in the War Office, it could not go by signal. I feel sure that you will see that it goes on safely and without delay.

I think you will find Martin the man you want. He is quiet and shy at first, but he really knows his stuff. He was more accurate than some of us about the probable run of events at Dieppe and he has been well in on the experiments with the latest barges and equipment which took place up in Scotland.

Let me have him back, please, as soon as the assault is over. He might bring some sardines with him - they are "on points" here!

Yours sincerely

Louis Mountbatten

Admiral of the Fleet Sir A.B. Cunningham, G.C.B.,D.S.O.,
Commander in Chief Mediterranean,
Allied Force H.Q.,
Algiers.

The letter from Lord Mountbatten

Now we come to the misleading documents. The letters hinting at the fake plans were going to be placed in a briefcase, which would be attached to the body by a chain, as it was impossible to rely on the body's hands continuing to grasp the handle of the briefcase. One letter placed in "Martin's" briefcase was from Admiral Lord Mountbatten, Chief of Combined Operations, who was in London. It was addressed to Sir Andrew Cunningham, in charge of our Navy in the Mediterranean, and based in Algiers. This letter explained that the contents of the other letter were so important it could not go by signal, but had to be delivered personally by a reliable officer. It went on to recommend the fictitious Major Martin as the ideal man to be entrusted with these secrets!

The other letter carried by "Major Martin" was from General Nye, Vice-Chief of the Imperial General Staff, to General Alexander, then in charge of our Army in Tunisia. The letter "explained" that our principal invading force would actually attack Greece, and that this plan was so Top Secret they did not wish to send it by wireless, but instead, were sending this trusted Major William Martin, to deliver the letter personally. Both letters were written and signed by the actual people, General Nye and Lord Mountbatten, who no doubt enjoyed this bit of skulduggery.

But if the Germans were going to be persuaded to believe the content of the letters, the man who delivered them would have to be given a convincing personal life.

The most obvious thing a young marine officer would have, would be a girlfriend. So two love letters were written to him by a fictitious fiancée "Pam", and then placed in his pocket. One of them rather neatly suggested that she was worried he might be going abroad, and hoping this rumour was not true! These letters were actually written by an MI5 clerk working in the same office as Montagu. Her name was Hester Leggett; she never married, and one colleague in the Office apparently found her "skinny and embittered". Yet the text of her letters has all the plausibility of a young woman in love, but desperately worried her fiancé is about to disappear abroad and, quite possibly, never come back. One just has to read her letters in a voice imitating Celia Johnson in *Brief Encounter* (another doomed romance), and "Pam's" personality comes brilliantly to life.

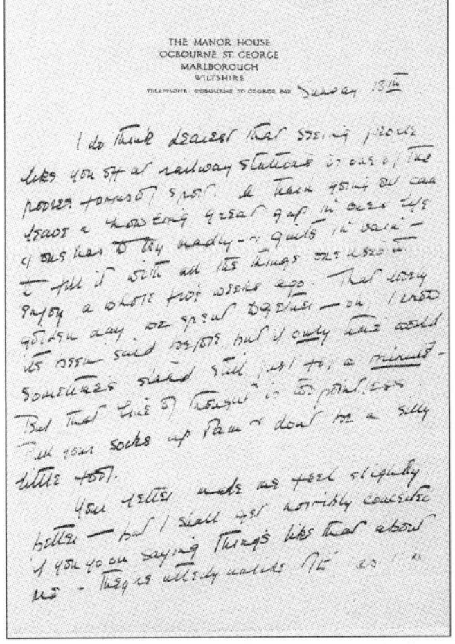
THE MANOR HOUSE
OGBOURNE ST. GEORGE
MARLBOROUGH
WILTSHIRE

Sunday 18th

I do think dearest that seeing people like you off at railway stations is one of the poorer forms of sport. A train going out can leave a howling great gap in one's life & one has to try madly – quite in vain – to fill it with all the things one used to enjoy a whole five weeks ago. That lovely golden day we spent together – oh I know it's been said before, but if only time could sometimes stand still just for a minute – But that line of thought is too pointless. Pull your socks up Pam & don't be a silly little fool.

Your letter made me feel slightly better – but I shall get horribly conceited if you go on saying things like that about [illegible]

One of Pam's two letters.

The second letter starts: *"The Bloodhound has left his kennel for half an hour, so here I am scribbling nonsense to you again. Your letter came this morning just as I was dashing out – madly late as usual! But what are these horrible dark hints you're throwing out about being sent off somewhere – of course I won't say a word to anyone – I never do when you tell me things, but it's not abroad is it? Because I won't have it, I WON'T, tell them so from me."*

It ends in a scribbled rush *"Here comes the Bloodhound, masses of love and a kiss from Pam."*

We shall probably never know whether Miss Leggett, as a young woman, had been in a similar situation to "Pam". But my mother remembered how many of her teachers at school in the 1930s had never married, because their boyfriends or, in many cases, fiancés, had been killed in the First World War. Hester Leggett may have had good reasons for her embitterment. If one war had ruined her chances of emotional happiness, she would do her best to ensure this new war was just a bit kinder in its results.

Left: The wartime photo of "Pam", actually Miss Jean Leslie and *right*, in 1996, when she was Mrs Jean Gerard Leigh.

The lady called "Pam" whose photo was used for the girlfriend came forward in 1996. She was Jean Leslie, later Mrs Jean Gerard-Leigh. The photo itself had been taken after swimming in the Thames near Wittenham Clumps, about nine miles south of Oxford. (The location was often painted by the war artist Paul Nash.) And it was, she remembered, "a very cold day."

The lady who took such a jaundiced view of Miss Leggett was, in fact, the same young woman who supplied the rather sexy photo of herself to go with the letters, purely to add plausibility, of course.

Among the other items in the briefcase were two theatre tickets for a performance two days earlier, a bill for the engagement ring for "Pam", a letter from his father about his marriage settlement, a letter from his solicitors about his Will, and a warning letter from his bank manager about his overdraft. The last two were written on official headed paper provided by the relevant businesses.

Although all this had been planned meticulously in advance, it had, of course, to be approved by those in authority. And that was where Montagu had the most difficulty with his superiors in the services. They all had different objections, but the principal one was that, if it went wrong and the Germans realised we were trying to mislead them, they would then realise that the target was actually Sicily.

Winston Churchill: a rare photo of him grinning: probably the expression he showed when all the details of Operation Mincemeat were explained to him.

Of course Churchill, as Prime Minister, had to be consulted on such an important plan. His answer to their objections was brief and to the point: "Anyone but a damn fool would *know* our target is Sicily!" So if the Germans realised this, no harm would be done. We would just face a furious fight when landing, which we expected to anyway. However, if the deception actually worked, it could save hundreds of lives.

Finally, when all had been prepared, they needed to get the body out to Spain, which seemed the most likely place for such plans to be leaked to the Nazis. They decided they should give the impression that Major Martin had been flying by plane on his "top secret" mission carrying letters to be delivered personally to the top brass in Africa. The Germans would assume his plane had been shot down at sea, resulting in his body being washed ashore on the coast of Spain. In practice, the body was going to be taken by submarine down to Spain,

The metal container, with the body inside, on the lorry driven up to Scotland.

and then placed overboard close to shore, where it would drift in, they hoped, to be picked up.

On 17th April 1943, Montagu and Cholmondeley took delivery of the body, which was encased in a large tubular metal container labelled "Special FOS Shipment: Optical Instruments". They were going to drive up to Scotland, as the submarine was based at Holy Loch. The man who shared the driving with Montagu was an MI5 driver, Jock Horsfall. That was Horsfall's daytime job, but in his spare time

Ewen Montagu *(left)* and Jock Horsfall beside the lorry carrying the body.

he was a successful racing driver. (He has a Memorial Trophy named after him, awarded every year at Silverstone.) For this job, Horsfall in fact provided his own van, with a tuned-up engine with which he claimed he had driven down the Mall at 100 mph! The 30cwt Fordson van was also customised to take an Aston Martin car in the back, when required, so the large metal container easily fitted.

The three of them: Montagu, Cholmondeley and Horsfall, drove to Scotland through the night. They took it in turns to sleep in the back, and arrived at Greenock Dock the following morning. The 400 lb canister was carefully lowered onto the deck of a launch, which took them out to meet the submarine. It was called the Seraph, and its commander was Lieutenant William Jewell. The container was placed aboard.

At 6 pm on 19th April 1943, the submarine Seraph set sail for Spain. They rounded Cape Vincent on 29th April, and on the 30th slipped the body into the sea, about a mile off the port of Huelva.

When the body arrived floating off the shore at Huelva, it was picked up by a Spanish fisherman, who handed it in to the Spanish naval authorities. As we expected, they informed a local German agent, who was allowed to copy the documents for his masters in Berlin. Soon after the body landed, the British made quite a fuss, once they were told about it, to make it look as they were indeed worried about the secret plans being found.

Some days later, the funeral was held for "William Martin", and he was buried in the local Catholic cemetery in Huelva.

The imposing gravestone in Huelva Cemetery: nearest the camera

Eventually, the British got the briefcase back, and it all looked completely untouched. Could it be the Germans had not even opened the briefcase and read the plans?

Luckily, our side had been careful enough to make sure there was only one fold in each of the documents they planted inside the briefcase. One of the documents they received back had two folds, one very close to the other, so the British knew it must have been opened, the Germans must have read it, and by extension, all the other documents too.

Our invasion of Sicily was launched on 10th July 1943, in appalling weather – rather like the launch of D-Day a year later. Yet, well before the 10th of July, there were signs that Mincemeat was having an effect.

At the end of May, a month after the finding of Major Martin, the German High Command ordered the laying of three new minefields off the coast of Greece. Hitler also ordered the 1st German Panzer (Tank) Group from France to Salonica in Greece.

In early June, a large group of German motor torpedo boats were sent from Sicily to the seas around Greece. Meanwhile, in the Western Mediterranean, a strong Panzer force with supplies for two months was sent, completely uselessly, to Corsica, and from now on there was repeated reinforcement of both Sardinia and Corsica. In Sardinia, German troops doubled to 10,000 by the end of June. In Greece, German forces were increased from one division to eight! And even two weeks after our invasion of Sicily, Hitler ordered his favourite General, Rommel, to take charge of the German forces in southern Greece. When it finally became clear we were not attacking Greece, Rommel had to be hurriedly sent from there to Italy. By that time, we had conquered Sicily, and had already invaded the Italian coast. Indeed, Mussolini had already fallen before Rommel even reached Italy!

All this movement of German forces away from Sicily was dramatically illustrated in the results. In our invasion of Sicily, the British Eighth Army expected 10,000 casualties in the first week. Just a tenth of that number were actually casualties. Meanwhile, the Navy thought it would lose 300 ships in the first two days alone. They actually lost twelve!

TWO

THOSE WHO TOOK PART

EWEN MONTAGU'S book *The Man Who Never Was* was published in 1953. Yet it took another forty years before we finally found out the identity of most of those who took part in the deception. The Official Secrets Act is still very powerful! It was when some of the files of the deception were made available to the public in 1996, that the historian Roger Morgan discovered the identity of the man whose body was used. He was revealed as Glyndwr Michael, a Welsh tramp, whose body was discovered in a warehouse. He had taken rat poison, either in suicide, or because he saw some bread lying around, and did not realise it had been poisoned. Although a lot of liquid was found in his lungs by the Spanish at the autopsy, this was assumed to have been swallowed when drowning.

Ben Macintyre is quite damning about the whole stratagem. "In one sense", he writes, "the story of Bill Martin was too perfect. There were no loose ends. A person's pockets and wallet will usually contain at least something that makes no obvious sense: an unidentified photo... (etc. etc.)" Well, yes, but "usually" does not mean "always". "The personal letters contain no spelling mistakes." But most reasonably well educated people will normally write letters without spelling mistakes.

The gravestone in Huelva, as it now looks. They added the name of Glyndwr Michael after 1996.

Macintyre continues, "There was excessive detail. Would Pam really bother to identify that she worked in a 'Government office'? Bill would surely know this."

Of course he would. But she was contrasting his exciting life, with hers, spent in a dreary office, and a Government one; likely to be twice as dreary. "Would a jeweller trouble to replicate the words engraved on a ring when sending in a bill?" They were actually letters and numbers, and yes, they are more likely to do so. Giving the exact letters and numbers engraved explains the then large sum of 10/6d for engraving thirteen of them.

Finally, he says, "In the warped intelligence mentality, something that looks perfect is probably a fake." But that's simply not true. The whole point of a deception operation is that every detail must fit. The chances are that, despite trying to think of everything, some trivial thing might still give away that deception is being used. One can only do one's best. As Macintyre admits, "The plot contained some potentially catastrophic mistakes. Martin left money to his batman. An officer in the Royal Marines would never have referred to a batman, but rather to his MOA." True, but he does not refer to his batman; it is his solicitor who refers to his batman, since that is what the solicitor would of thought of him as being. "Why did he pay cash for his shirts when he was deeply overdrawn and owed £53 for an engagement ring?" For the obvious reason that, in that state of indebtedness, the shop would give him no further credit, and insisted on cash.

Lastly, Macintyre complains that there were loose ends not tied up. One was, he wrote, that there was no entry in the visitor's book for Major Martin's (equally fictitious) father having stayed at the Black Lion Hotel in Mold, Wales. Within a week of Macintyre's book being published, he got a phone call from Wales telling him that, in the old visitors' book of the Hotel, there actually is an entry recording an apparent visit of Mr Martin Senior. Montagu and his colleagues really had thought of virtually everything.

The logic of saying a story is "too perfect", is to make some deliberate mistakes in a deception, so the "warped intelligence minds" can then say, "It must be genuine, because it has mistakes in it." For example, one double-agent Eddie Chapman, as Agent Zigzag, did make one mistake. In telling his tale of carrying a briefcase with an explosive charge on the left hand side, when he told the same tale a week later, he mentioned the charge was on the right hand side. At once, his interrogator pounced on the discrepancy and demanded an explanation. Thinking very quickly, Chapman said, "Yes, I had one explosive charge on the left side, and another on the right side." He is hardly likely to say, "Ah yes, I deliberately got that detail wrong, because otherwise, you might think my story was too perfect!"

The plot of Operation Mincemeat was not "too perfect": it was as good as they could make it at the time, and, as we have seen, it worked.

THREE

SIR JOHN MASTERMAN AND THE DOUBLE CROSS COMMITTEE

Sir John Masterman, aged 61, painted by Edward Halliday. The painting hangs in Worcester College Hall. Reproduced by kind permission of the Provost and Fellows of Worcester College Oxford.

ALL THE DECEPTION plans were co-ordinated by the XX – i.e. Double Cross – Committee, a Sub-Committee of MI5, which was chaired by J.C. Masterman. It was sometimes called the Twenty Committee, because XX means "twenty" in roman numerals. He had been an undergraduate at Worcester College Oxford, before the First World War, then a history don at Christ Church between the Wars, before being co-opted into MI5 during the Second World War. Just after the War, he was elected Provost of Worcester College, Oxford. He retired from this post in 1961, when Lord Franks became Provost, and he then went to live in a flat in Beaumont Street, just down the road from Worcester. Since my father knew Masterman during the War, this was one of the reasons why I chose to apply to Worcester when I went to Oxford. While I was there, from 1966 to 1970, my father wrote to Sir John, and I went to visit him in his rooms, probably in 1967.

He was interested to know what my father was doing now, so I told him that, having been co-opted into MI5 during the war, he had never moved far from it. My father had asked the family to keep quiet about his being in MI5, but Sir John was so eminent and reliable, I felt it would have been ridiculous to be cagey in his case.

Sir John said he had been hoping to publish his own version about the whole programme of deception during the Second World War. However, he said he had not yet managed to get authority from senior officials to do so. The story of his efforts to be allowed to do so is told in his autobiography *On the Chariot Wheel* (1975). It was in October 1967 that he embarked on his final effort to publish it: the same year that I met him. The actual book, which he had written as an internal report at the end of the War, was finally published in 1972 as *The Double-Cross System in the War of 1939 to 1945*. What should have been an exciting narrative is, I am afraid, not very exciting. While he gives the bald facts, that is what they come over as: a factual narrative. Ewan Montagu, by contrast, had to get agents to play a part skilfully and imaginatively. With his barrister's training, he knew just how to tell a story in an exciting way, as he does in his book. A barrister needs to tell a narrative convincingly – whether or not it is true.

When I asked Sir John how Ewen Montagu had been allowed to publish his book so soon after the War, he said Montagu had been very cunning. He had asked various senior officials what they thought. They all said they would not object if X, Y or Z did not object. So although no-one officially gave him the go-ahead, no-one actually forbade it either, and that was enough for him to take the risk and publish. He must have been influenced by the fact that he was no longer in MI5 – indeed, he had become a prominent barrister and QC. So although he was still officially bound by the Official Secrets Act, he clearly felt no harm would be done by revealing this individual story – and indeed, no such harm was done. When Masterman wanted to publish his book, he would be revealing the basic details of all counter-espionage during the War, and this might have been more prejudicial to future security ventures.

There was, however, a curious sequel to this conversation with him. On one occasion in 1970 I was talking to the then Vice-Provost of Worcester College, and former Tutor in Law, Alan Brown. I must have been discussing *The Man Who Never Was* with him. Brown then said that the only time he saw John Masterman really furious, was when Montagu published his book. But his fury, he said, was

The first Corgi edition of *The Man Who Never Was* by Ewen Montagu

because Montagu took all the credit for devising the scheme himself, when in fact it was he, Masterman, who had thought up the whole idea!

This is curious, because in Masterman's book he discusses TMWNW in about two pages, gives the impression that Montagu and one other were in charge of it, and that the XX Committee (which Masterman chaired) kept an eye on the project. In fact, all our sources, released more recently, show that the George mentioned was actually Fl Lt Charles Cholmondeley.

But was it perhaps Masterman who devised the scheme as it was finally carried out, with Montagu being the officer who carried out his instructions? There is no evidence of that either. Despite devoting several pages of his book "The Double-Cross System" to TMWNW, he nowhere claims any part of the devising of the plan – giving all the credit to the two officers.

A photo of Masterman, sitting on the steps which lead up from the garden to the Provosts' Lodge at Worcester College. He used it on the cover of his autobiography.

Masterman's historical writing can be rather dry, one has to admit. On the other hand, he did write a very good detective story called *An Oxford Tragedy.* So he did have the right sort of imagination for convoluted plots. It seems more likely that Mr Brown simply witnessed how cross Masterman was, that Montagu could actually get commissioned to produce his own version of a true deception story, while Masterman could not get permission to publish his own, already written, story of Deception throughout the Second World War.

Perhaps Masterman felt he should have been given some credit for chairing the XX Committee. But Montagu could not reveal this in the 1950s. It was up to Sir John in his own publication of *The Double-Cross System* to do so, in 1972. It is curious that he does not. He says he wrote this report immediately after the War. So why did he fail to update this part, nearly thirty years later, with more details of how he helped in the scheme and, in particular, how he had chaired the Committee? His publishers should have pressed him on this, since that fact clearly adds to the authority of the book. Anyway, the habit of secrecy dies hard, and perhaps Masterman felt he could not or should not step out from anonymity for his book, despite being tempted. By 1975 he had changed his mind, and finally revealed his Chairmanship, hidden away on page 222 of *On the Chariot Wheel* (1975).

A still from the 1956 film *The Man Who Never Was*; Ewen Montagu, *right*, had a small part as an Air Vice-Marshall; the American actor Clifton Webb, *left*, plays Montagu.

The title *The Man Who Never Was* was actually invented by the News Editor of the Sunday Express, Jack Garbutt. The Express had serialised the story in 1953, and the complete book with that title was published soon after. When the film came to be made in 1956, the American actor Clifton Webb played Montagu, and Maurice Denham was also in the cast. Curiously, the voice of Winston Churchill in the film was provided by Peter Sellers.

While the film was being made, at least two of those involved in the original deception were called in for advice. Cholmondeley was there in the background, called George by everyone. But my father told me that he too was involved in the making of the film. He said originally the makers of the film asked him to type various messages in Morse code, filmed his hand doing so, and were going to use the sound of the tapping as well. In the film, the message being typed and sent to Berlin was "Martin genuine", but this whole section of the film was invented for dramatic reasons. The director later decided to dub Morse-like music over the sound of the tapping, though as far as I know, it is my father's hand which is seen tapping the Morse!

The cleverest use of music to symbolise Morse was the incidental music for the Inspector Morse series, which was set in Oxford. Barrington Pheloung wrote the signature theme, which starts with a musical version of Morse being tapped out. It is of course a pun on the Inspector's name.

Part of Worcester College, Oxford, 2010 The Nuffield Building is on the right; my own room in 1968 had the top window between the two chimneys at far left, part of the 14th century cottages.

My father's other memory of Worcester College, other than working with Sir John, was of attending a conference there in the late 40s or early 1950s. In particular, he remembered attending a meeting in the Nuffield Building. I therefore wrote to my old College to see if they had any record of such a conference. It turns out they have records of at least three such conferences, in 1948, 49 and 50. They also have the correspondence referring to them. I quote from Emma Gudrun, the College Archivist.

"A quick internet search has revealed that James Fulton, who wrote the letter dated 14th September 1949, worked for the Secret Intelligence Service around this time, and I assume that he is referring to the SIS and the Security Service when he states that "such meetings help both the services get to know their opposite numbers under very congenial conditions." The same letter thanks "J.C." for his and the College's hospitality, and refers to "Sinbad's absence on leave". Miss Gudrun points out that "Sinbad" was the nickname of Sir John

Alexander Sinclair, who worked for the SIS from 1946, and was Chief from 1953 to 1956. Among those listed as attending are Lt-Col Robertson, the "Tar" Robertson who was in charge of the XX project during the War, and Brigadier White, who went on to become head of SIS.

Sir Karl Popper, a guest at the weekend.

Also attending, for one night, was Professor Karl Popper, author of the influential "The Open Society and its Enemies", and Professor of Logic and Scientific Method at the London School of Economics. Since both MI5 and SIS were established to protect us from "enemies of the state", his presence there seems entirely appropriate

As well as correspondence with Sir John, the College have lists of those attending the conferences in 1948 and 1950: a total of 55 in each year. Strangely, there is no mention of Major Reed attending either conference. However, in 1950 there is a record of a "Major Martin" attending the conference. My father always had a slight twinkle in his eye when he mentioned the conference he attended. Could this have been because, when attending, he used the name of the man he had impersonated, the Man who Never Was?

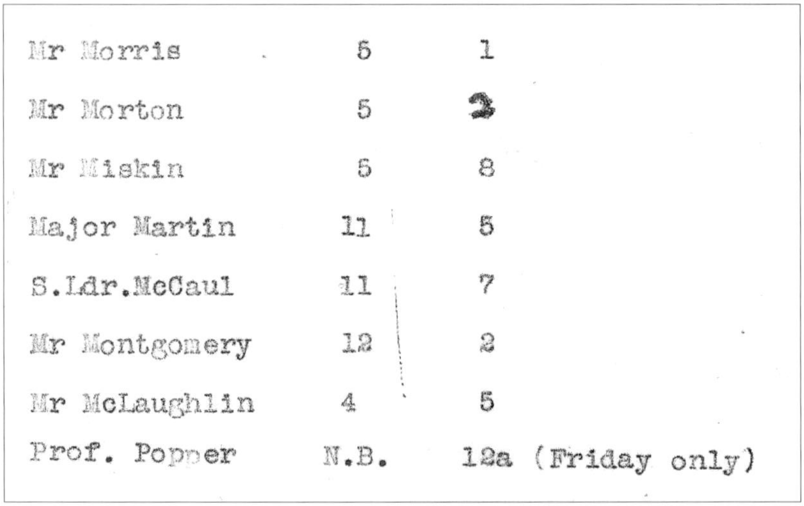

Mr Morris	5	1
Mr Morton	5	3
Mr Miskin	5	8
Major Martin	11	5
S.Ldr.McCaul	11	7
Mr Montgomery	12	2
Mr McLaughlin	4	5
Prof. Popper	N.B.	12a (Friday only)

A detail from the attendance list for 15th-18th September, 1950. "Major Martin" was, it seems, staying in Staircase 11, Room 5. Prof Popper stayed in the Nuffield Building.

FOUR

THE SERAPH

All photos in this chapter are from The Citadel Archives and Museum, Charleston, South Carolina.

The crest, taken from the Seraph

THE SUBMARINE called the *Seraph*, which was used to carry the body down to Spain, had already been used for two other difficult and dangerous missions. In 1942, commanded by the 29-year-old Lieutenant Bill Jewell, the ship's mission was to deliver the American General Mark Clark, deputy to Eisenhower, onto the North African coast, to meet some French commanders in Algeria. The French forces already in Algeria might have gone over to the German side, if their Vichy commanders decided to. But we were about to invade Africa, and it was vitally important to try to persuade the French to stay neutral for the moment. So the Americans, with three British marines, landed just after midnight, met the French negotiators and talked through the night. Shortly before dawn, they were betrayed, and had to make a run for it, under fire, to reach the boats which could take them back to the *Seraph*. They succeeded, just.

In March 2011, a small group of Britons landed in the Libyan desert, by helicopter, in the middle of the night. With a senior British diplomat guarded by several marines, they were captured by local

The Dedication Ceremony for the *Seraph* monument: held on 2nd November 1963, seen from above (*left*), and from the ground (*right*). Note that the American and British flags fly side by side at equal height: the only place in America where this is allowed.

militia, and finally ejected from the country. Were they trying the same trick as in 1942, but this time attempting to lessen the danger for the civilian who landed in Africa? It may be years before we find out.

In two further missions in 1942, Lieutenant Jewell continued to captain the Seraph. Its next mission, curiously, once again involved the French and the Americans. This time they were to pick up a French officer, General Giraud, from hiding with the resistance in the south of France, and deliver him to the French forces in Africa. He was thought most likely to bring the French forces over to join the allied side. However, his boss, General de Gaulle, decided that only the Americans should be allowed to rescue Giraud. The reason why de Gaulle and Giraud detested the British was that, at Churchill's orders, once the Nazis had overrun France, the British had destroyed the French fleet, for fear that the French ships might be captured and used by the Nazis. As a result, de Gaulle decided that Giraud could only be rescued by an American, not a British, vessel. So, for this mission, the Seraph now flew the Stars and Stripes, and an American Captain, Jerauld Wright, was placed in nominal command of the ship. Indeed, for a time she had two captains and operated under two flags. Once Giraud was transferred to the ship, all the British crew adopted American accents, and hoped Giraud would be convinced. He probably saw through this stratagem, but turned a blind eye to it.

In December 1942, the Seraph was sent on a further secret mission: to reconnoitre the volcanic island of Galita, 80 miles off the coast of Tunisia. They were to see if it was suitable for attack by American commandoes, to be led by Colonel William Darby of the US Rangers. (The American 1st Ranger Battalion was the nearest equivalent to the British Royal Marine Commandoes.)

Darby must have been almost unique in turning down promotion three times, so that he could stay in battle leading his troops. It was he who joined the Seraph for this reconnaissance, and photographed the beaches of Galita for two days. Eventually, though the island turned out to be suitable for attack, it was decided there was no tactical advantage in capturing the island – it was not on the way to Sicily – and it was left alone.

The monument during the dedication ceremony, 2nd November 1963

After the War, General Mark Clark became President of The Citadel, the Military College of South Carolina, USA. Although the *Seraph* was broken up, he was among those who ensured that several parts of it were removed and rescued. These included heretofore hatch, ship's bell and badge, periscope, and her flag: the Ensign of the Royal Navy. These parts of the ship were then erected and dedicated in the grounds of The Citadel. So this is the only place in the world where the two flags fly side by side, as a monument to Anglo-American understanding.

However, another flag is also preserved from the *Seraph*. Curiously it is the pirate flag, the Jolly Roger. Lieutenant Jewell used to fly it, once they were back in harbour, as a symbol of success in another of his buccaneering adventures. Since most of his missions had been both dangerous and secret, it was presumably a relief to get back safely and announce one's presence in a striking way.

Given the importance of Anglo-American understanding, both during the War, and ever since, it is surprising there is no regular ceremony to mark its importance. Something should surely be arranged to mark the 50th anniversary of the dedication of the *Seraph* monument. This will be on 2nd November 2013.

The Jolly Roger, as flown on the *Seraph*.

The ship's wheel, with the periscope above.

FIVE

Prelude
RONNIE'S FATHER, THOMAS REED

OUR STORY begins at Kensington Parish Church in 1883, when Robert John Reed, aged 31, married Sarah Little, aged 26, from St Leonards-on-Sea. Robert's grand address of 16 Hyde Park Gate is misleading: he was a butler, and so probably lived in. His father George had been a publican; her father James had been a carpenter, but both were already deceased by the time of their children's marriage. By 1886, perhaps when Robert had a new employer, the couple were living at 43 Hyde Park Gate Stables. They went on to have two sons and two daughters. Their elder son was called Robert J., after his father. On 23rd August 1889, they had a second son: Thomas George Reed: my grandfather. However, within three years the father and bread-winner, Robert Reed, had died, in March 1892, aged 39. This left Sarah Reed a widow, with four children under the age of seven. It is good to know that she was able to remarry fairly soon, having found someone who would take on not just her, but her four children as well. She married James Oliver in December 1894.

We next find Thomas in Sandgate, near Folkestone in Kent. In the census of 1901, aged 12, he was staying at 3 Victoria Terrace, a brick-built weather-boarded terrace house close to the church at Sandgate. He was a boarder there with his elder brother Robert, not with their mother but with another family. His mother, meanwhile, had moved to No 3 Martello Terrace, Sandgate. This is about half a mile away, in Castle Road, close to Sandgate Castle.

The prize book presented to Thomas Reed.

At the age of 13, Thomas won a prize, which was presented to him at Christmas 1902, at the Sunday School at St Paul's Church. One assumes that Thomas himself chose what book he would like as his prize, and it was the vicar Mr Eustace Bryan who presented it to him. It was *20,000 Leagues under the Sea*, by Jules Verne.

Jules Verne was the world's first science fiction writer, and he was of course French. But at this point, it is worth diverting from our narrative to talk about Britain's first and most famous science fiction writer: HG Wells.

In September 1898 Wells, suffering from a serious kidney complaint, was advised by his doctor to move from Worcester Park to the coast. Wells had already written *The Time Machine* and *The War of the Worlds.* Both books quickly became popular and well-known, so Wells' arrival in Sandgate must have created a sensation in this little village. He moved into 2 Beach Cottage, facing the beach at Sandgate. The house is visible from Martello Terrace, where Thomas Reed's mother was living. Six months later, Wells moved round the corner, to Arnold House, 20 Castle Road, immediately opposite the local church school which the young Thomas Reed was attending. Wells was there for two years, and then moved to the grand house he commissioned from the architect Voysey: Wells House, just up the hill from Castle Road. It is still there, as an old people's home.

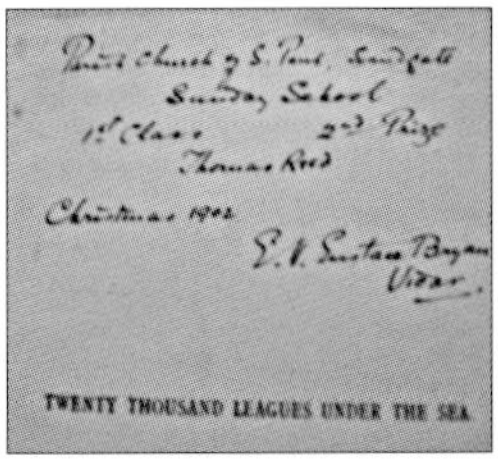

The inscription inside the book.

So it is probably not just a coincidence that, when Thomas Reed had to choose a book as a prize, he chose a book of science fiction. Was Thomas, as a schoolboy, daring enough to approach the great man on some occasion? Did he perhaps tell him how he enjoyed *Time Machine*, much the most famous of Wells' short stories, and which Thomas (who was clearly interested in science fiction) is bound to have read? It would be nice to imagine that he did, and that Wells recommended another science fiction writer to him: his great predecessor, Jules Verne. HG Wells is going to crop up again in our narrative, when we come to Thomas's son.

The Reed family in about 1910, with young Thomas sitting on the arm of the chair next to his mother.

In about 1910, the Reed family must have gathered in the family home in Sandgate, and then went into Folkestone to have their photo taken to commemorate the occasion. They commissioned the top Folkestone photographer, Hawksworth Wheeler, to take it. Wheeler is now best known for his archetypal photo of the soldiers setting off for war down the Slope Road in Folkestone (later called the Road of Remembrance). No doubt Wheeler posed the family in the back garden of his photographic premises in Church Street. And that is where we see them: Robert Reed, Thomas's elder brother, standing at the back, his mother Sarah in a chair at left, and young Thomas resting on the arm of the chair beside his mother. Thomas's two sisters, Edie and Foundy, are seen in smart white dresses. As everyone is very well dressed, one wonders if this was a special occasion. If Edie or Foundy had just got married, we would expect to see their husband in the photo. But it was, for what it's worth, the year in which Thomas had his 21st Birthday. In this, the earliest photo we have of Thomas, he does not yet have the neat moustache which he grew soon after.

The front entrance of the Trocadero in about 1910.

Once he had finished school, he went off to London, and within a few years, he had become Deputy Head Waiter at the Trocadero. This was one of the grandest restaurants in London at the time. It stood in Shaftesbury Avenue, where the rebuilt Trocadero complex now stands. Opened in 1896, it was the grandest of the various establishments founded by J. Lyons and Co. In 1901, for the funeral of Queen Victoria, army officers all dined at The Troc, as it was known. In 1905 several motor car enthusiasts met at the Trocadero and decided to set up the Automobile Association. Its original objective was, not to help motorists who had broken down, but to warn them of speed traps.

At the Troc, Thomas Reed had at least two close friends who were also working there: Auguste Velluet and Gerald Clapham. He kept in touch with them when he became a soldier. And, as we shall see, he sets off to France with "Jerry", which must be Gerald Clapham.

Thomas and Theresa Reed at about the time of their wedding.

Sometime in 1908 he met Theresa Barrett. When I interviewed her in 1971, she could not remember how they met – possibly at a dance. But they courted for seven years, and finally married at their local parish church, St Pancras, in 1915. A year later, on 8th October 1916, their son, Ronald Thomas Reed, was born.

Thomas smiling broadly, on his way to France. (From the *Folkestone Herald* newspaper).

When war broke out in 1914, Thomas joined his local regiment, the 4th East Kent regiment, known as "The Buffs". His work as a Head Waiter meant he was the ideal sort of man to be valet to a senior officer, and by 1917 he was orderly or valet to Lt. Col. Vaughan-Cowell, of the Berkshire Yeomanry, working in the Officers' Mess in Dedham, Essex. So for three years all his military service was back in England, far away from the action in France.

Finally he was sent to France, at his request. We see a broad smile on his face, in a photo taken shortly before he set off. In September 1917 we find he has left his usual barracks, and is on his way south. He sent a letter from the Officers' Mess of the Buffs, at the Musketry Camp at Sandwich. It reads:

"My Dearest Terry,

Have got to Sandwich allright. Had to march it, as Jerry and I missed train this morning by five minutes. I'm chiefly writing this to let you know my address. I think the above will find me allright. Shall be here, I think, till Friday.

Have heard heavy gun fire lately. I hope it is only the gun practice from Dover. Excuse scribble as I am writing under difficulties. All my love to you, darlings.

From Your Ever Loving Tommy XXXXXXX"

Once enlisted for France, he started to keep a diary, with short entries. The first entry is for 26th September 1917, "Left Bourne Park Camp 4.15am. Arrived at Southampton Docks."

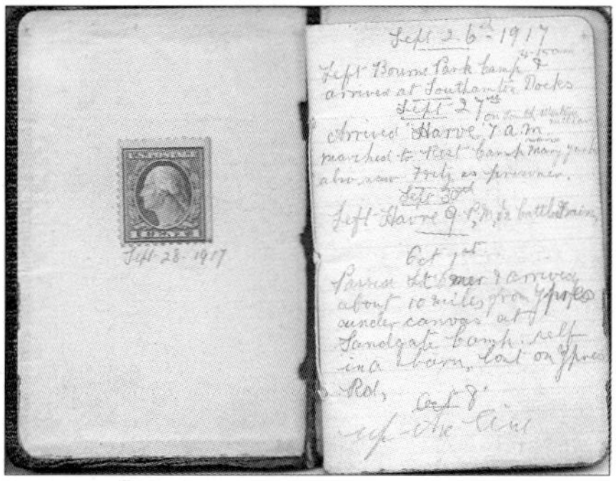

Thomas's diary for Sept/Oct 1917, with the green US stamp.

On 27th September, "Arrived Harve 7am". Clearly "Harve" was the English term for Le Havre, as "Wipers" was for Ypres. He spells it correctly in the next entry. He continues, "Marched to rest camp. Saw many Yanks. Also saw Fritz as prisoner." Fritz was the slang term for Germans.

He stays in the rest camp for the next three days, when he must have talked to some of the "many Yanks", because inside the diary he has stuck a green US one cent stamp showing George Washington. He carefully dated it 28th September 1917.

On 30th September he records, "Left Havre 9 pm, in battle train".

The last detailed entry is for 1st October. "Passed St Omer and arrived about 10 miles from Ypres. Under canvas at Sandgate Camp".

Sandgate Camp would have been one of the many such camps in France, given familiar English names. But how nice he was in one named after his native town: perhaps he had some choice in going there. He finishes "Self in a barn, lost on Ypres Road." No doubt this was to remind him of a more detailed story he could have told on his return. The final entry is for October 8th. Hastily scrawled are the words, "Up the line". And there his diary finishes.

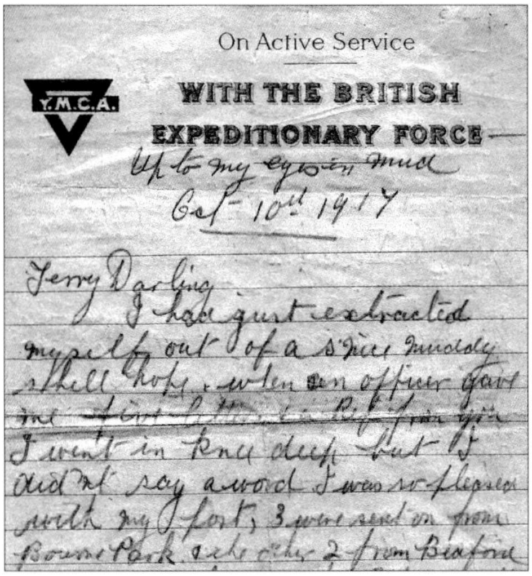
On Active Service

Y.M.C.A.

WITH THE BRITISH
EXPEDITIONARY FORCE

Up to my eyes in mud
Oct 10th 1917

Terry Darling
I have just extracted
myself out of a nice muddy
shell hole, when an officer gave
me five letters & a Ref from you
I went in knee deep but I
didn't say a word I was so pleased
with my post, 3 were sent on from
Bourne Park & the other 2 from Bedford

The first page of his letter of 10th October 1917.

But these were not the last words he wrote. Two days later, he wrote a letter to his wife: the only such detailed letter to survive from his hand. It is of historical interest, both as an account written in the trenches, and as the only detailed example of the writing of the father of Ronnie Reed, so I quote it in full. The single sheet has the printed heading "On Active Service With the British Expeditionary Force".

He starts graphically, "Up to my eyes in mud," with the date underneath: Oct. 10th 1917. I should explain that, in his letter, the word "Ref" must be a reference to the newspaper called the Referee, which was published up till 1939.

"Terry Darling, I had just extracted myself out of a nice muddy shell hole, when an officer gave me five letters and a Ref from you. I went in knee deep, but I didn't say a word. I was so pleased with my post. 3 were sent on from Bourne Park and the other 2 from Bedford. One letter contains the Ref as well. I was very glad to hear you are feeling better for the change of air(raids). According to Mrs Velluet's letter she properly got wind up. But I know dear it must be rotten if one's nerves cannot stick it.

You might send me an envelope and paper in each letter, dear. That pad was no good – would not stick. A few home made cakes now and again dear would be very nice and a couple of candles, also a Sunday paper. I think the Despach *as I have not time to read the Ref article. Please send me a paper of Oct 10th just to see how things went.*

I shall be very pleased with the watch dear. Give Foundy my love and thank her very much. I am still very fit and very fed up with this game. I hope Ron has got his birthday present allright. I was glad to hear his cold was better.

As to food, dear, I shall never look at a biscuit again, but I don't do so bad. I hope Mrs Collis and all are well, dear. I have not heard any more of Frank yet, but I know he is round this way somewhere. The boys all send kindest regards to you.

Love to all. In haste for? Censor. All my love, Tommy."

This was the last letter she received from him, and after three weeks Terry wrote in great anxiety to find news of him. By this time she had moved out from Leigh Street to Bedford. As mentioned in Tom's letter, this was because she was very distressed by the German air-raids over London. She seems to have written two letters enquiring about him. One was to the Officer Commanding the 4th (Reserve) Battalion of The Buffs. He replied on 6th November, writing from Crowborough, that he had no information, but was forwarding her letter to the Colonel in charge of Records no 2, at Hounslow. Hounslow replied on 20th November, saying they had heard he had been wounded in action. They then sent their letter to Terry' old address in Leigh Street, so of course it did not reach her till December! But she had also written to the British Red Cross Society. This was forwarded to the War Office, and their letter of 3rd November did reach her in Bedford, telling her he had been wounded.

On 3rd November, after nearly three weeks of no news, Lieutenant-Colonel Vaughan-Cowell wrote from the Berkshire Yeomanry HQ at Dedham, Essex. He was clearly writing in response to a worried letter from Terry, pleading for more news of her wounded husband. He said, "I have just received your letter, and am sorry to say that your information is correct. I heard from one of my officers the other day, saying that your husband was wounded at the same time as Lieut. Mitchell, and I am afraid that both were badly hit. I will get some more information and write tomorrow. I was *extremely* sorry to lose Reed, but it was his wish that he should go with Clapham and Velluet rather than go to the Reserve Battalion and be drafted out without his friends." And there is this mention of the two friends with whom Thomas worked at The Trocadero, and whom he wished to join at the front.

This letter does not seem to have reached Theresa Reed until late in November. In fact, she heard of Tom's death through a relative, rather than through official channels. What she received was a telegram from her elder sister Edie. It was sent on 2nd November, and presumably reached Terry within a couple of days. Edie said she had had a "Letter from Len telling me the worst had happened and that he had written to you. Try to be brave, dear. Edie." So this was Terry's first news of Thomas: clearly implying not just that he was wounded, but that he was dead.

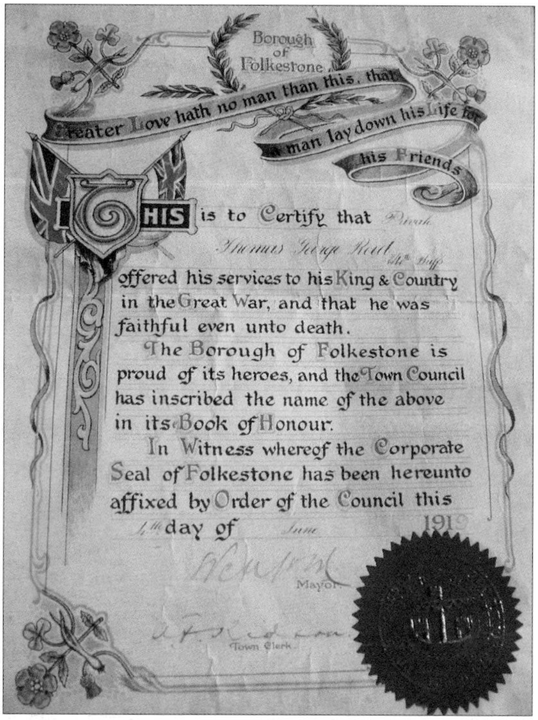
Borough of Folkestone

Greater Love hath no man than this, that a man lay down his Life for his Friends.

THIS is to Certify that

offered his services to his King & Country in the Great War, and that he was faithful even unto death.

The Borough of Folkestone is proud of its heroes, and the Town Council has inscribed the name of the above in its Book of Honour.

In Witness whereof the Corporate Seal of Folkestone has been hereunto affixed by Order of the Council this day of 191

Mayor

Town Clerk

The Certificate from the Borough of Folkestone, saying that the Borough was proud of its heroes, and that the Town Council had inscribed his name in its Book of Honour.

True to his promise, Col Cowell wrote again the following day, 4th November. He prefaced his remarks by saying: *"I know no more distressing job of a commanding officer than that of acquainting people with bad news. I have had a letter from my late adjutant, in which he tells that your husband was very badly hit by a shell and that he was not expected to survive his serious wounds. I now understand that he died in the Field Ambulance on October 13th. It is with the deepest regret that I give you this news. My opinion of him as a soldier and a man was the highest I could hold of anyone. Nothing was too much for him either in my service or in the Officers' Mess. I have written to the Managing Director of the Trocadero about him and you."*

At least those who had worked with Thomas expressed real sympathy. This was shown not just by Col Cowell, but also in a letter from Lt G S Dixon, writing from the 4th Buffs, attached RGLI (Royal Guernsey Light Infantry), BEF (British Expeditionary Force), France. He wrote on 30th October,

"It is with very deep regret that I have to inform you that your husband has died of wounds. I received notification from England today in a letter from the Battalion orderly room of the 2/4 Buffs...Your husband went up the line with his company and they were rather heavily shelled. The same shell that wounded your husband killed the company commander (a cutting of whose death I enclose), wounded Lt Mitchell, the officer

to whom your husband was servant, wounded your husband in the stomach and also several others. Immediate assistance was rendered and your husband was taken to the advanced dressing station. After that nothing more was heard of him, although we sent round to the casualty clearing stations in the area without result, and the letter I received yesterday was the first news we had of him. As I was adjutant of the late 2/4 Buffs I knew your husband pretty well, and I should like to take this opportunity of informing you what a splendid man and cheerful soldier he was. He was very popular with all the officers and men of the old Battalion, and nobody could speak too highly of him. Both in England and in France he did his duty as a man and has died in the service of his country.

"All the officers and men of the 2/4 Buffs who are attached to the Royal Guernsey Light Infantry out here, wish me to offer you their most sincere sympathies in your great loss."

Thomas Reed at Kennington, near Ashford, Kent December 1916.

According to my father, Tom had ambitions eventually to retire from London and run a smallholding in the country. Indeed, there is a photo of him taken apparently on just such a smallholding, surrounded by chickens, with a look of enjoyment on his face. It is dated 20th December 1916, and was taken at Kennington. Almost certainly he was on Christmas leave, and he and his wife went back to Sandgate to see his mother. They must have had friends at Kennington, which means this is likely to be the village just north of Ashford in Kent. From the thick black belt visible round his waist, which is presumably his military belt of webbing, one assumes he is in uniform, but has rolled up his sleeves to help in feeding the chickens. So here we see him, holding a can, presumably of chickenfeed, and perhaps thinking ahead to doing something similar when the War is over.

This is the only photo we have of him smiling, apart from the one published in the paper announcing his death. That second smile was presumably because the photo was taken after he had just heard that he was going to be sent to France, when he could join his friends from the Trocadero, who were already out there. His friends both survived the War: indeed Auguste Velluet lived to a ripe old age. His grandson Paul Velluet, now a senior officer of English Heritage, remembers meeting him in the 1960s. But of course they did not discuss the First World War: few veterans did in those days.

Back on April 10th 1917, presumably when Thomas was serving in Essex, he sent a couple of dried poppies in an envelope, with two short notes inside. The notes were made from one sheet of ruled exercise book paper – probably the only sort of paper around at the time. The first says, "For my Dearest Terry. With all her Tommy's fondest Love, hoping to be with you again quite soon. xxxxxxx". The other is, "For my Dearest Sonnie. With all Dad's fondest Love, trusting he will be a good boy to Mum till Dad returns. Xxxxxxxxx". But Tommy was not to return. He died almost exactly on the first birthday of his only son. Thomas George Reed was buried in Solferino Farm Military Cemetery, Brielen, about two miles north-west of Ypres.

Dedication of the Sandgate War Memorial, 11th November 1923.

But that is not the only place he is recorded. On the 11th of November 1923, the new War Memorial was consecrated at Sandgate. A postcard survives of the occasion. It was sent by Tom's mother Sarah to Theresa, her daughter-in-law. The card shows a big crowd gathered round the Memorial, the vicar conspicuous in his white robes, and in the foreground, three ladies in cloche hats looking at the camera. On the back of the postcard, Sarah Oliver (Tom's mother) writes, "Do you see my old face?" The one on the left seems to be Sarah. By this time her husband had died, and she had remarried, to a Mr Oliver. Her card starts by asking "Is it my fault you don't write? You was going to let me know about (the) jacket." I presume Sarah was asking Terry if she wanted to have Tom's old jacket which he must have left at Martello Terrace.

An Order of Service survives with the postcard, and is presumably the one followed in 1923. The first poem read was *For the Fallen*, by Lawrence Binyon, which includes the immortal lines "Age shall not weary them, nor the years condemn. At the going down of the sun, and in the morning, we shall remember them." The second was *In Flanders Fields*, by Lt-Col John McCrae, MD. It ends, "If ye break faith with us who die, We shall not sleep, though poppies grow In Flanders fields."

And last, the Recessional Hymn, by Rudyard Kipling, with its chilling refrain, "Lord God of Hosts, be with us yet: Lest we forget – Lest we forget!"

In fact, we do have several other memorabilia kept by Terry. The saddest is a wallet in which Terry kept his letters to her, and she kept his diary, and her later correspondence, from which I have been quoting. But the wallet must have been returned by the War Office after Tom's death. When they returned it, it still had his blood splashed on it: a thoughtlessly callous thing to send it back like that. I remember my father speaking quite bitterly about how inappropriate he thought it of them to have sent it to her. They also sent to her the identity tag worn by all serving soldiers, and similarly bloody. My father placed with it in the wallet the identity tag which he was given to wear during his service in the Second World War. Such dog-tags were worn by all serving soldiers, to identify the body in case it was difficult to recognise.

Thomas's death was only finally announced in the *Folkestone Herald* in February 1918. The announcement said he had "died of wounds", but that was not in the field of battle. My grandmother remembered that in fact, before he had got to the front line, a stray shell came over and wiped out six of them. More pointless waste of life. Eventually his widow received the large ornamental certificate recording the nation's

Gnr. L. R. CAREY, R.G.A.; gassed. Husband of Mrs. Carey, 64, Mead-road.

Pte. T. G. REED, "Buffs"; died of wounds. Son of Mrs. Oliver, 3, Martello-cottages.

Part of the Obituaries column of the *Folkestone Herald*, 9th February 1918.

gratitude toward those who had died in the service of their country. There is also a large bronze medallion inscribed with his name.

After the War, Sarah continued to live in Sandgate. On July 28th 1927, she went up to The Guildhall (Photographic) Studio in Guildhall Street, Folkestone, and had two photographs taken, on what was her 70th birthday. We see one of them below.

Sarah Oliver, Tom's mother, aged 70.

Sarah Oliver was still living at Martello Terrace, Sandgate, in the 1930s. In 1996 I interviewed an elderly resident, Mrs Champion, who remembered her, and three things about her. She always kept her hair neat; she was proud of her jewellery, and she had a small flower garden she looked after carefully. So this was someone remembering details about my great-grandmother, who had died sixty years earlier! It's never too late to start asking questions about family history.

Sarah's widowed daughter-in-law, Theresa, continued to live at 9 Leigh Street, St Pancras, with her small son, Ronnie. And it is he who is really the subject of this book.

SIX

RONNIE REED: EARLY LIFE

RONALD THOMAS REED was born on 8th October, 1916, almost exactly a year before his father was killed in France. Throughout his youth, he and his mother Terry lived in a flat on the top floor of no 9 Leigh Street, just off the Euston Road. On one occasion Ronnie reminisced how, along Euston Road, there had been large gardens in the centre of the road, in which the children played. As Euston Road was widened for traffic, these gardens got increasingly smaller, until they were finally replaced by the six or eight carriageways which now carry the thundering traffic.

Our first glimpse of Ronald, as a baby, is when his aunt Edie, sister of his father Thomas, wrote to young Ron two days before his second birthday, on Sunday 6th October 1918. She began, "My darling little man, Aunty is writing to you today, ready for your birthday on Tuesday. Aunty, Uncle and Bunty all send you lots of love and kisses dear, and wish you ever so many happy returns of the day. We hope that you will soon grow up to a great big boy, and always look after and love Mummie, and Aunty hopes it won't be long before you can have Mummie with you all day long." Presumably Terry had to go back to work during the week, to supplement her meagre War Window's pension, and young Ron complained that he missed her.

"I am sending you some money, and Mummie must take you up to Mr Cox's money shop [the local bank], and then buy you something nice, and herself a box of powder, which Aunty forgets every time she goes out. Thank mummie for her letter. I should love to hear you sing "Roses in Picardy" and "Goodbyee". So here we catch a glimpse of young Ron singing these two songs from the First World War, when he was only two.

I refer to him here as "Ron" because that is what his mother called him throughout his life. But when he grew older, he changed his name to the more neutral "Ronnie", which could be middle as well as working class. This decision was reinforced when my mother met him. In the 1960s radio show *Take it from Here*, June Whitfield played the part of "Eth", who had been engaged for seven years to Ron Glum. His father was a publican, played by Jimmy Edwards. Each episode started with Eth saying "Ohw Ron", and then trying not to be too desperate in putting up with her fiancée Ron, who was played by Dick Bentley as utterly gormless. At least, by being called "Ronnie", Ronnie Reed could avoid being associated with that character!

Ronnie looking smart in white flannels, when aged about 12.

Ronnie went to St Pancras Church of England School, Thanet Street. In my 1994 interview with him, my father summarised this in one sentence. "I went to school at a church school near where we lived in Leigh Street, not far from Russell Square." Luckily, we have a vivid account of life at the School from Charles Chilton, who was a contemporary of Ronnie at the School. Charles went on to be a BBC Radio producer, and is now best remembered for a radio play he wrote, which was adapted into the musical called *Oh What a Lovely War*. This was first seen as a play produced by Joan Littlewood, and then the 1969 film directed by Richard Attenborough, and filmed on the old West Pier at Brighton.

A photo of Empire Day at Thanet Street School in about 1928.

Charles writes about Thanet Street School as follows:

"The large photo is of one of the Empire Day Pageants which we seemed to perform every year. The legend behind this pageant "Here and here did England help me…" is somewhat ironic for I remember at the time I wore no socks and had shoes that literally had no soles to them. I was virtually barefooted. There were two or three of us in similar circumstances.

As each year came round, we, being a year older, were given more important parts to play. I can remember the year of the enclosed photograph quite well – though not the date, but it must have been the late twenties. In this edition, I was one of the four Saxons who were dressed in white smocks. We fought the Normans who were dressed in crusader style and carried shields with red crosses painted on them. I am in the picture – second row under the "A" of "can". Ronald (what we can see of him) appears to be a Saxon too, but as he was older than me and always in the class above me I hardly think he would have played such a small role. The girl playing Britannia is Mona Hofer who became the famous model. Her father was German, which led to her and her mother having a rough time from neighbours during the First World War. I took her to a performance of my (and Joan Littlewood's) play *Oh What a Lovely War*. She burst into tears during the Christmas in the Trenches scene where the German and British soldiers befriended each other. Her father had died soon after the war."

The photo below shows a group of the children on a ramble. According to a contemporary cutting, "A party of the school children spent a happy afternoon in Metroland, rambling from Uxbridge to Denham for a picnic tea."

Thanet Street schoolchildren rambling in Metroland. Among those seen are Charles Chilton, wearing a cap at the back on the left. Next to him is Mona Hofer, wearing a cloche hat, and in front of her is Ronnie Reed, also wearing a cap.

"The School Report", said Charles, " brought back many memories. I can remember Ronald being made to take his work (Geometry it was) round to the rest of us to show us how it should be done. He always seemed to be top at exam time. I did not take the same exams as he because they were different for the lower classes. I did get a first on one or two occasions but always in the second year when I had been through the syllabus twice. This has stayed with me. I never seemed to accomplish anything until I've had two goes at it."

Two of Ronnie's school reports survive, from 1926 and 1927. In 1926 he came second in a class of 35; in 1927, in a class of 46, he came top. The comment from his class teacher Mr Richardson was "An excellent worker hence position of excellence on Class List. Very neat and conscientious in all his work."

School Report.

Charles continued, "*Play the Game* was a bit of a laugh really. Such a school motto was the result of W.H. White, the headmaster, having weird ideas of trying to turn a Church of England elementary school into some kind of Eton or Harrow. We had to learn *Play The Game* (Newboldt). He also tried to get the pupils to wear school uniforms, mainly a peaked cap and special blazer. A number of parents could not afford such luxuries so did not buy them. So caps and blazers were offered on easy weekly repayments. This was something my grandmother understood. She ordered the cap and blazer. But I wore them only once, after which they were pawned in order that we might have a Sunday dinner – and they were never redeemed. So far as I know no payment for them was ever made. Instead my grandmother "took in" the school's weekly washing (mainly towels and dusters) at a special cheap rate. This seemed to be satisfactory. White's real desire was to be a priest. We had a chapel in the school where we were compelled to attend Eucharist; the full sung version. I learned to sing it with my eyes shut and, later, while reading a copy of *The Wizard* folded into the music book. We were not taught to read music but learned the Eucharist by rote. I think White had quite an influence in persuading some of the boys of Thanet Street School to join the St Pancras church choir. Ronald was a prominent member – and soloist.

"The Scotch Church played an important part in my life but not in Ronald's. Ronald and his friend Bill Sanglier favoured Boy Scouts. There was a troop attached to St Pancras Church which used to meet in the basement of the Thanet Street School. The Scotch church boasted a Boys Brigade Company complete with drum and fife and bugle band which suited me better. It was with them that I first learned to read music."

St. Pancras Church

St Pancras (New) Church was consecrated in 1822, and designed by William and Henry Inwood. It has two porches on either side, one facing Euston Road. The roof of each is held up by sculptures of ladies, sculpted by John Rossi. These were clearly inspired by the Caryatids in the portico of the Erechtheum, which stands near the Parthenon on the Acropolis in Athens. The tower of the church is also copied from the Tower of the Winds in the Agora in Athens.

Charles Chilton mentions that Ronnie probably joined this Church under the influence of his headmaster. He adds, "The church was often heard over the air, for it was fairly regularly attended by the (then)

St Pancras Church; the grand front entrance.

Sir John Reith, Director General of the BBC. I was quite unaware of this until some years after he had resigned from the BBC."

Ronnie sang in the choir at the church, having quite a good treble voice, and there is a recording of him and another boy treble singing a duet with organ. This was in the days of the young boy treble Ernest Lough and his recording of Purcell's *Oh, for the wings of a dove*,

The Four Caryatids holding up the roof of one of the porches at St Pancras Church

Ronnie and his mother on Hampstead Heath in the early 1930s. At that time he had a dog: it was his wife Mary who won him over to cats.

which became an immensely popular recording, much like Aled Jones in more recent times. According to Charles, Ronnie had hopes he might be chosen as the soloist for the recording, but that was not to be.

Ronnie also became a 'server' at the Church, and recalled what he had to do as a 'server'. During the service, he would stand next to the vicar with the wine, ready for the blessing of the bread and the wine. My father would estimate the number of people in the congregation, and then pour into the chalice the amount of wine which seemed to be needed for that number of people. However, if the vicar nodded to him, he had to pour more wine into the chalice. At most services, the vicar nodded several times, and my father duly poured out substantially more than would be expected for the congregation. The secret lay in the fact that, once that wine was consecrated, it could not of course be thrown away. Any wine left over, had to be finished by the vicar himself. No doubt he was conscientious in doing so.

Ronnie told me that, as a teenager, he had some trouble with the idea that God was all-seeing, because, as he asked the vicar, "Does that mean that He sees me when I am in the toilet?" The vicar reassured him about this. (Perhaps he told him that The Lord always averts His eyes, when we go to the loo.) But Ronnie's doubts about religion really began when he asked the vicar about some of the texts in the Old Testament which he and the choristers sang regularly. For example, in the Psalms, the writer talks about smiting the enemies of the Lord, smiting them in their thousands even unto the third generation. As my father said, this was not easy to reconcile with the idea of an all-loving God, who believed we could be forgiven, despite our sins. The unsatisfactory answers he got from the vicar on this point, were what really turned him away from Christianity and towards agnosticism.

The term agnostic, of course, describes someone who says he genuinely does not know whether there is a God or not. It comes from Greek, and literally means "not knowing". The Latin verb for the word is "ignoro", from which we get the word "ignorant". There is a story of one young man who applied for Oxford, and in his application form, under Religion, rather daringly put "agnostic". The don who was interviewing him referred to this and said, "Young Man: in this college we use the Latin language. Would you kindly correct the word to "Ignoramus".

Amateur Radio

An interest in radio showed itself early in both Ronnie and Charles: Ronnie in fact built himself an early form of citizens' band radio, and used to experiment by talking to Charlie on this (illegal) form of communication. The neighbours all knew, because their radio programmes were frequently broken into by Ronnie calling up his friend on their home-made set. As Charles recalled later, neighbours dreamily listening to Victor Sylvester on the wireless would have their listening rudely interrupted by a loud voice saying, "Can you hear me, Charlie?" Ironically, Ronnie went to some trouble in later years to write and complain about the presence of local pirate radio stations in his part of London. In the 1980s and 90s, these frequently interfered with the radio signal of Classic FM.

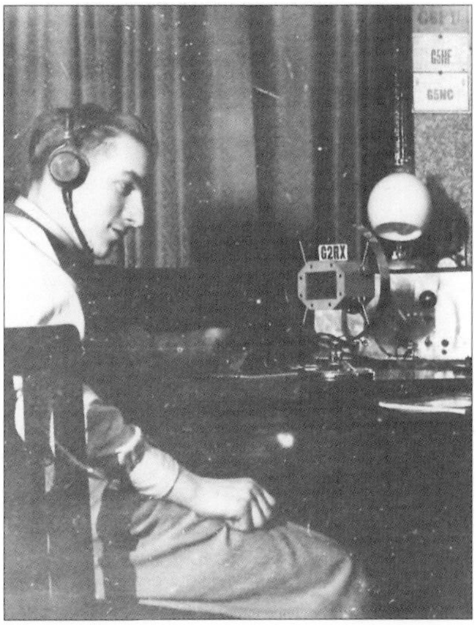

Ronnie with his earliest amateur radio equipment in about 1932, when he was sixteen. Note the early microphone in front of him.

This interest in electronics was shared by many others at the time. According to Professor R.V. Jones (of whom we shall hear more later), "My main hobby in my schooldays was, as with many other boys of my generation, the making of radio receiving sets. [Ronnie was six years younger than Jones]. There has never been anything comparable in any other period of history to the impact of radio on the ordinary individual in the 1920s. It was the product of some of the most imaginative developments that have ever occurred in physics, and it was as near magic as anyone could conceive in that, with a few mainly home-made components simply connected together, one could conjure speech and music out of the air. The construction of radio receivers was just within the competence of the average man, who could thus write himself a passport to countries he could never hope to visit. And he could always make modifications that might improve his aerial or his receiver and give him something

Above: Regent Street Polytechnic on the left, probably shortly before the First World War. In the distance can be seen the church of All Souls, Langham Place. As this church backed onto the BBC, the Corporation quite often broadcast Choral Evensong from there. *Right:* Detail from a panoramic photo of the Polytechnic Secondary School taken in 1929. Ronnie, aged 12, is circled. In 1965 Travel Polytechnic joined up with Lunn Travel to become Lunn Poly.

to boast about to his friends. I acquired much of my manipulative skill through building and handling receivers. When at last I could afford a thermionic valve in 1928, I built a receiver that picked up transmissions from Melbourne, which that station acknowledged by sending me a postcard carrying the signatures of the English Test Team."

My father's reminiscences continued, "I got a scholarship from there (the School) to Regent Street Polytechnic, which was considered to be a great school at the time, run by Quentin Hogg, and I stayed there until I was sixteen or so. "

The Quintin Hogg he refers to, set up the Polytechnic in the 1880s. He was the grandfather of the Quintin Hogg who was Lord Chancellor under Mrs Thatcher. In 1896, the Polytechnic Theatre was the venue for the UK's first ever public display of moving pictures.

It was Ronnie's cousin Jeff Peel, who told me of one ambition Ronnie had in his early days. Later on in the interview, Ronnie mentions his collection of jazz records. But he also had an almost complete collection of 78rpm records of Bing Crosby singing. It seems that Ronnie thought he might be able to have a career as a singer of light music. I don't know how far he took this, though there are photos he had taken, which attempt to show him as a type of matinee idol – and with his good looks that was not difficult. One or two private recordings survive of Ronnie singing popular songs. Indeed, Charles Chilton remembers Ronnie doing a very fair imitation of Bing Crosby singing, while Charles accompanied Ronnie on his guitar! It seems

Above: the matinee idol, as he hoped to be. Taken in 1937, he was just 21.
Right: just strolling along: the next Bing Crosby?

possible that Ronnie's introduction to music through singing in the church choir, made him wonder if he could continue singing as an adult. Charles Chilton remembers him hoping to be the child who was recorded singing *Oh for the Wings of a Dove* by Purcell. The child who won that competition, Ernest Lough, went on to national fame as a result.

Ronnie did in fact continue as an amateur tenor, and in his later years sometimes attended weekend courses in singing.

Ronnie briefly described what happened when he left the Polytechnic. "it seemed to me, my mother being a war widow, my Father having been killed only a few months after I was born, it was a bit hard for her to try to keep me, so I wanted to get out and do something. I looked round for various jobs, having no particular qualification except the usual O Levels or equivalent."

The Missing Years 1933-38

In his interview, Ronnie went on, "The change came really, from what I was doing, in about 1933," and described how he came to join the BBC. However, he mentioned he was 22 at the time. That dates it to 1938, not 1933, and that is confirmed by the date of the ad in which the BBC job was advertised. So what was he doing between 1933 and 38?

This shows Ronnie in overalls, with a workmate, and looking younger than when he was in the BBC. It presumably shows him at work, gaining his experience, during those missing years.

The archivist at Regent Street Polytechnic found his name at the Poly from 1929, when he was in Form 3, to 1933, when he was in the Lower 6th. But there is no mention of him at the Poly after that. Nor is there any mention, either of him winning prizes, or even of him matriculating in 1933 or 34, either in external or internal examinations. Perhaps he obtained a City and Guilds qualification elsewhere. In fact my brother tells me that he worked somewhere else between 1933 and 1938, because my father kept in touch with someone from that workplace until his death in 1995. By the time I heard about that person and rang them, the number was unobtainable, and I think they too had died. But it must have been in that job, presumably to do with radio engineering, that Ronnie had "learned a lot", as he put it when describing how he was accepted by the BBC.

Ronnie Reed, just visible top left, with friends in the 1930s. Probably fellow members of the Radio Society of Great Britain, which Ronnie joined in 1933. Two of them wear headphones, and there is a microphone inside the tent.

SEVEN

WORKING FOR THE BBC 1938-40

RONNIE CONTINUED: "The change came really from what I was doing, when an uncle of mine who lived in Nottingham sent me a cutting from a newspaper. He said that he'd seen that the BBC were advertising for young maintenance engineers who could be sent anywhere round in the country to be trained in all the experiences of the BBC. I had taken an interest in amateur radio for a long time, had no real scientific qualifications, but I learned a lot. So when I went to my interview with the BBC, to my surprise they were quite prepared to accept me, together with five other young men all aged 22 – like Dennis Horsfall, with whom I'm still in touch, who lives in America. They said they were going to send us round the country to get experience of the BBC and its engineering projects. We were going to be looked upon as – wonderful title – "Floating Staff - Junior Maintenance Engineer". And as we were all unattached, we could be sent anywhere at a moment's notice. So they first sent me to the Glasgow Empire Exhibition '38 where I did a stint there – great fun.

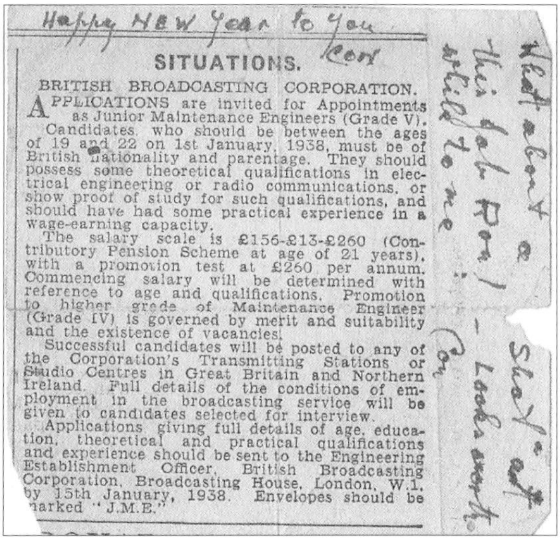

Happy NEW Year to you Con

SITUATIONS.

BRITISH BROADCASTING CORPORATION.

APPLICATIONS are invited for Appointments as Junior Maintenance Engineers (Grade V). Candidates, who should be between the ages of 19 and 22 on 1st January, 1938, must be of British nationality and parentage. They should possess some theoretical qualifications in electrical engineering or radio communications, or show proof of study for such qualifications, and should have had some practical experience in a wage-earning capacity.

The salary scale is £156-£13-£260 (Contributory Pension Scheme at age of 21 years), with a promotion test at £260 per annum. Commencing salary will be determined with reference to age and qualifications. Promotion to higher grade of Maintenance Engineer (Grade IV) is governed by merit and suitability and the existence of vacancies.

Successful candidates will be posted to any of the Corporation's Transmitting Stations or Studio Centres in Great Britain and Northern Ireland. Full details of the conditions of employment in the broadcasting service will be given to candidates selected for interview.

Applications giving full details of age, education, theoretical and practical qualifications and experience should be sent to the Engineering Establishment Officer, British Broadcasting Corporation, Broadcasting House, London, W.1, by 15th January, 1938. Envelopes should be marked "J.M.E."

What about a shot at this job Ron! - Looks worthwhile to me : Con

Above: Ronnie photographed in Glasgow in 1938, at the start of his contract with the BBC. Note that he now has a small moustache, rather like Errol Flynn or Clark Gable. The larger moustaches probably became more common once handlebar moustaches became almost a badge of rank in the RAF!

At *right*, the advertisement which his Uncle Conrad sent to him in January 1938. His uncle adds, "What about a shot at this job, Ron? Looks worthwhile to me. Con."

These are two postcards of the Glasgow Exhibition which my father kept. Both show the magnificent Art Deco buildings which featured at the Exhibition. The tall thin tower visible on the far left of the photo above, was called the Tower of Empire, and was 300 feet high.

The Glasgow Empire Exhibition was held in Bellahouston Park from May to October 1938. It was the second Empire Exhibition in Britain: the first was the better-known one held in Wembley in 1924. The architect for Glasgow, Thomas Smith Tate, produced his plan for it in February 1937, and the whole exhibition, with 150 buildings, was complete when it opened in May 1938.

All the buildings were modern, but many also modernist and art deco in type. Ronnie was clearly very impressed by it, and his interest in architecture remained later in life. Indeed, he used to write to Prince Charles's Trust to comment on modern buildings, and I remember him saying how much more sensible the Sainsbury Wing was as an extension to the National Gallery, than the "monstrous carbuncle" originally planned on that site, to which Prince Charles had famously objected. He also bought a copy of the book Charles wrote about modern architecture and his work at Poundbury.

The new studios in Glasgow, as featured in a one-page article from the *Listener*, published on 17th November 1938. The short man nearest the window, wearing headphones, looks exactly like my father, which may help to explain why he kept the cutting.

Those who have seen the film *The King's Speech* will be aware that King George VI's most testing experience, after receiving therapy for his stammer, was giving a speech at the opening of the Glasgow Exhibition. It follows that the sound engineer who arranged the radio microphone to pick up the speech for broadcasting to the nation, may well have been my father.

The Glasgow Exhibition was the largest exhibition in the world up to that time, covering five acres, and its tallest building was a skyscraper 300 feet high. It had more fountains and water displays than ever before, and fantastic lighting displays, shown in the evening, as the exhibition stayed open till 11pm at night. During its six months, it welcomed twelve million visitors. Three buildings remain from it. The Palace of Art building is still there in the park, while two other large buildings were later rebuilt near Scottish airports.

My father's interview continued: "Learned a lot about Scotland and Glasgow. I had lodgings in Sauchiehall Street with an inebriate Irish woman whose husband was a ship's engineer. He used to come home and beat her up frequently, when I got no breakfast or meals for a couple of days until she recovered. It was also a theatrical lodging house, so we had chorus girls and all sorts of other people staying there.

This meant that you had to hide behind your door in order to listen for the click clock of the bathroom, in order to get in there in the morning, as they were always washing their nylons (or the equivalent). So I had six months in Glasgow and then six months at Bournemouth, with a very old fashioned transmitter. I stayed in Oxford Road with a Welsh landlady. There were four of us by that time – two others had gone somewhere else. Then I was transferred to London, to Broadcasting House – outside broadcasts."

Among the photos Ronnie kept, is this professionally taken large photograph (below), folded in a cardboard mount. As usual with Ronnie's photos, there is nothing written on the back of the photo or its mount. However, the front flap of the card has a woman's head in semi-profile, embossed in a flowery way. It looks to me like a representation of Ariel, the sprite who "could put a girdle round the earth in forty minutes." Once wireless was in operation, it could, of course, girdle the earth in far less than forty minutes. So the BBC adopted the spirit of Ariel as their emblem, and their staff newsletter is still called *Ariel.*

I went on to ask him, "Do you remember any particular things you did on outside broadcasts?" He replied, "Concerts at the Queens Hall – well of course the Queens Hall has now gone – and all sorts of other concerts. At outside broadcasts in Southampton, we used to

In this photo, Ronnie is visible seated at the front, third from the right. As there are 33 young men in the photo, one wonders if they are the entire "year of '38" at the BBC.

A detail from the photo on the previous page. Ronnie is the middle of the three shown. One can see that he has a light-coloured tie, unlike any of his contemporaries, and appears to have a corduroy or possibly velvet jacket. In other words, he is trying to stand out from the crowd, and dressed more in the way one might expect of a matinee idol.

do concerts of chamber orchestras from the ballroom and all sorts of interesting projects like that."

(*NR: "What about one or two of your colleagues at the BBC, because Charles Chilton was one of them?"*) Yes: he was very interested in records. Charles – with whom I was at school with my Primary School – Charles became very well known for American Jazz and being an expert on American Jazz. He used give me all the spare records from the BBC they decided they didn't want, so I have a great pile of 78 rpm records of famous jazz pianists and singers and trumpeters – recordings thrown out from the BBC."

(*NR: You also knew Lance Sieveking?*) "No: I remember him being a producer there. (*This was BBC radio?*) This was BBC radio: that's right (*NR: But you'd built your own television, hadn't you?*) I had built a Baird television set on which you had a flickering image on the screen. That was quite interesting, and the disc which you used – a large disc with forty very small pinholes around – is now in use again by a man who lives, I think, somewhere in Forest Hill, who reconstructed one of the 1936 Baird televisors. And I had had that disc on the wall for some 50 years and gave it to him, in order to finish off the job." My father later explained to me that he had been listening in to a chat between two "hams", with the one saying to the other that he had built a complete Baird TV system, but the only thing he didn't have was the disc which got it to work.

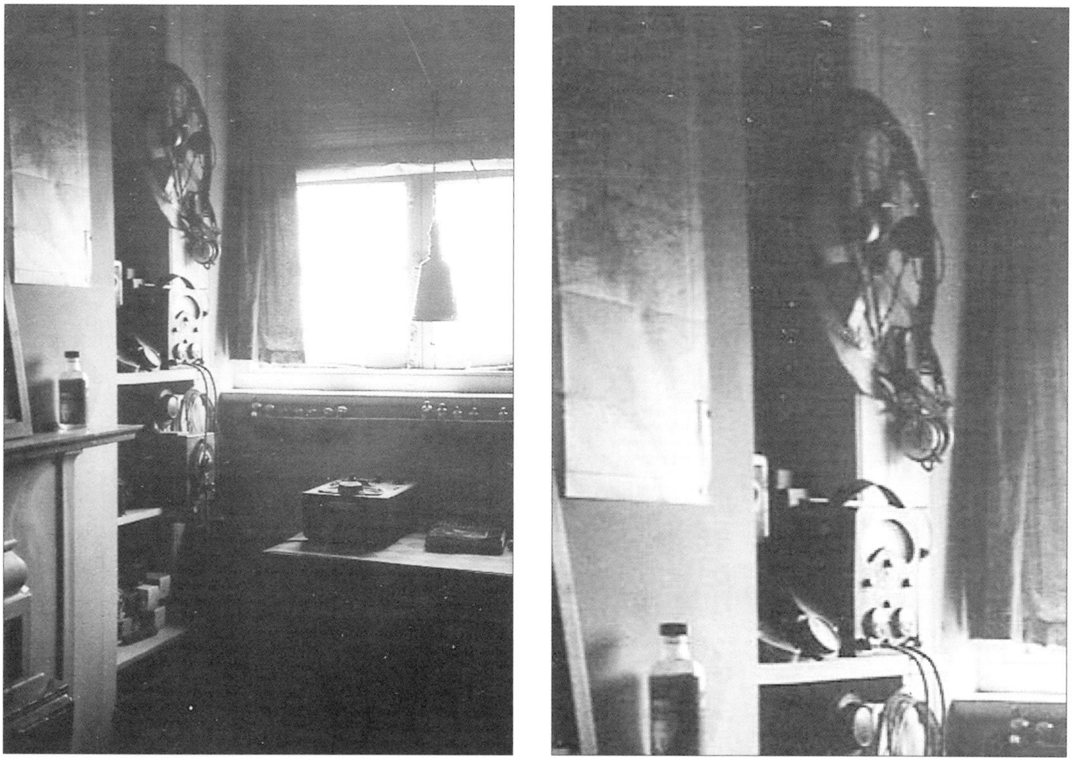

Ronnie's radio "shack" at Dulwich in the 1960s. In the detail (right) can be seen the large disc he refers to, hanging on the wall, with headphones hung on top of it. I think the instrument seen at the bottom was used to measure voltage.

Ronnie kept up his interests in electronics at home: built his own television in about 1932, and also gained the call sign G2RX as an amateur radio ham in the same year. He made his last contact with a fellow amateur radio friend on 6th January 1995, having made his first such call in 1933: a total of 62 years as a radio ham. The man he spoke to, Kenneth Moreton-Evans, was to be a colleague of his in the Office during and after the War.

9, LEIGH STREET, LONDON, W.C.1
ENGLAND.

TO RADIO...
Confirming our QSO at......................GMT/BST on..................193....

UR SIGS were
QSA......... R ....
QSB to R.... .. ..
Tone T....................
On Rx.....................

G2RX

QRH................Mc band

XMITTER
....
Input............ Watts
AERIAL....................

Remarks ....

Vy 73 es DX OM. hpe CUAGN.
Op. R. T. REED.

PSE QSL: Direct or via R.S.G.B.
Print by G6DS

Left: his first printed QSL card, i.e. the card he would send to other radio hams after they had made contact. They would reply with a similar QSL card. This one has his home address in Leigh Street, where he lived with his mother.

EIGHT

THE FIRST DOUBLE-AGENTS, BEFORE CHAPMAN

AS AN AMATEUR, Ronnie had joined the Radio Society of Great Britain in 1933. When the Second World War began, the RSGB suggested its members should join the Radio Security Service. Those who joined it, were asked to monitor the airwaves for possible illegal transmissions. So his radio skills were known to the authorities, and that is no doubt why they asked for his help.

His article on "Technical Problems Affecting Radio Communications by the Double-Cross Agents" (see Sources) starts by writing about the first double-agent active in Britain in the Second World War.

"*Snow* was the first agent to communicate with the Germans by radio, soon after the outbreak of war in 1939. [*He was a Welshman whose real name was Arthur Owens. NR*] His radio set was installed in a cell in Wandsworth prison where he had been detained under DR 18B. The radio was operated by a warder who knew the Morse code, although the Germans assumed it was *Snow* himself who was transmitting. The warder also listened around on his receiver and reported that, noticing the style of the operator in Germany and the characteristic Morse note of the transmitter, he recognised that communications were taking place at times other than when Snow was on the air. This gave our intercept stations a most important clue to the German spy communications network in Europe."

"The first spy to bring a radio set with him was *Summer* who landed by parachute not far from Aylesbury on 6 September 1940. He was captured within a few hours of landing, interrogated and revealed his code and instructions. An immediate attempt was made to establish communication with the Germans."

Summer was actually a Swiss citizen named Goesta Caroli, and was the first agent that my father met, as described below.

We take up the story with the article which my father wrote for the in-house magazine of MI5, which is called *Portcullis.*

"Most of us remember the seventh of September 1940 as the day the London docks were bombed and devastated by fire. I remember it as the day I was called up. At the time I was an engineer at the BBC. I was one of half a dozen unattached young men who had been

Broadcasting House is the gleaming white building behind. This shows it soon after its opening in 1932. In front is All Souls, Langham Place, from which concerts were often relayed.

recruited in 1938 under the title "Junior Maintenance Engineer – Floating Staff". Then aged 20-22, we were taken on to be trained in the technical aspects of transmitters, studios, control rooms and outside broadcasting and told to be ready to be posted anywhere in the UK at a moment's notice, to fill unexpected vacancies – hence "floating staff".

A German attack on the London docks. The day the Germans switched from bombing airfields, to bombing London, was 7th September 1940: the start of The Blitz.
Right: A milkman resumes his rounds, surrounded by devastation.

Ronnie's special pass for the BBC Control Room

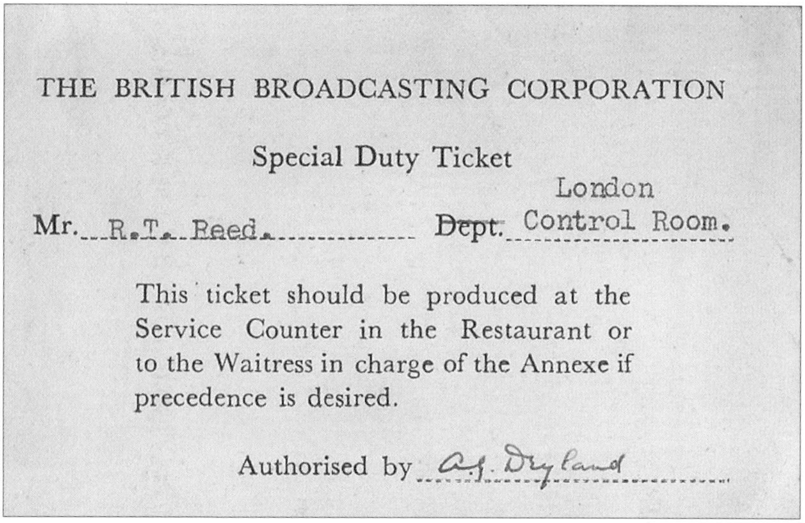

THE BRITISH BROADCASTING CORPORATION

Special Duty Ticket

Mr. R. T. Reed. Dept. London Control Room.

This ticket should be produced at the Service Counter in the Restaurant or to the Waitress in charge of the Annexe if precedence is desired.

Authorised by A. J. Dryland

"I had been on duty during the day in the control room at Broadcasting House. When the building was designed, the control room was placed on the top floor, but on the outbreak of war, it had been relocated well below ground level. I was living in north London with my mother and on arriving home, with the bombing increasing over the London docks, we made our way to the Anderson shelter in the garden. *[His address at this time is recorded on a calling card as 78 Lady Margaret Road, Tufnell Park N19.]*

"At about 9.30pm I heard a car draw up. A policeman put his head into the shelter and said "I am looking for a Mr Reed". When I replied "That's me", he said, "I want you to come with us, Sir". When I asked why, he replied, "You will find out when you get to the Police Station at Kentish Town". On arrival there, I was asked to ring the Head of Overseas Engineering, Mr Hayes, who was waiting for my call. He said to me, "I cannot tell you any more than that the Police will take you to where you have to go. I suggest you pack a bag as you may be away for some time." I was taken home, picked up a bag and tried to calm my mother. I said I hoped I would be able to keep in touch.

The front entrance of Wormwood Scrubs Prison. Wormwood Scrubs was in fact where MI5 was based for the first part of the War.

In the police car we sped westwards under reddening skies and anti-

An inside view of the landings and cells in the Prison, as Ronnie would have seen them.

aircraft gunfire. When I asked where we were going, my police escort would only answer "I am sorry. I can't tell you that." At about 11 pm we pulled up in front of a pair of large wooden doors. I recognised the place as Wormwood Scrubs from pictures I had seen – not from previous experience. After ringing the bell a small wicket gate was opened and a man introduced himself as Reggie Gibbs. He thanked the police for finding me and asked me to follow him. We walked through a dimly lit prison block and up some iron stairs. Stopping at a cell door he pushed it open and said "In there, please". It was the only time I faltered. "In there?" I asked. "Yes".

"So I went in. In front of me was Colonel Warledge in red tabs, Malcolm Cumming, one or two others and a dishevelled civilian with congealed blood on his forehead. He was standing in front of a portable radio transmitter on the table. I was told, "This man is a German parachute spy. He was dropped from an aircraft at Aylesbury a few hours ago and has to transmit a Morse message tonight. We have prepared one and want you to go with him to Aylesbury where we will set up the transmitter. You must listen to him carefully to be sure that he sends only the message we have agreed".

"Cars appeared. A police escort in front with the spy, a van for monitoring purposes and Malcolm and me fetching up the rear. We drove through the night, to the house of the Chief Constable, who said we would transmit from the field where he had a pigsty where we could string up the aerial. The spy and I lay on the ground while he, white-faced, sent his message and I monitored the Morse.

"It was a coded message in five letter codes. Having accomplished that, we weren't quite sure whether we'd got through, because we

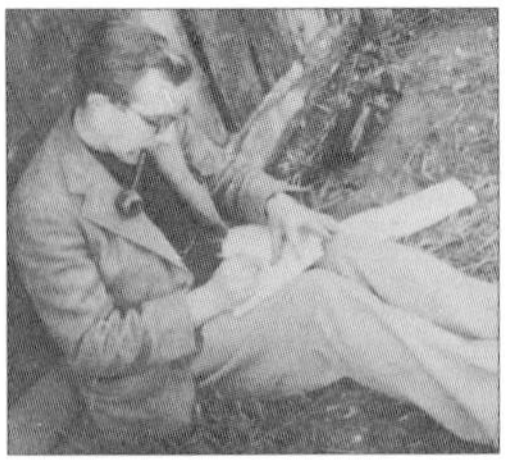

Three views of Ronnie operating a set in the field.

This building, which looks like a barn, may be the Chief Constable's pigsty near Aylesbury.

didn't get the acknowledgement. But it was the right time and the right frequency, and we came back to London, where I was put up in a cell at Wormwood Scrubs.

"We were going to repeat the procedure the next night, and I said, "Well, from the point of view of distance, it won't make a lot of difference whether it's in the pigsty or in the Police Station, because the direction-finding won't show it. I think we'd be much more comfortable in the Police Station, and I'll be able to fix up a transmitter properly, with the aerial, so we know it's working. That evening we transmitted the same message. The chap had said in the coded message, "I'm going underground for a few days, while I sort out some accommodation, but I've arrived safely." This time we got a reply from Hamburg, saying "Message Received and Understood."

My father continued: "He was the first of four German parachute spies who came to this country, and were taken to a place called Camp 020, which was in Petersham, near Ham Common. It is now a historic house, I think." *(Actually it is still (2011) a prison, but is now called Latchmere House. In 2004 it was described as the "best prison in the country at providing useful work for its inmates." NR)*

Latchmere House, Petersham

"They had turned it into a prison for captured spies, who were told that they could either cooperate with the British authorities, or be executed. What would they prefer? *(NR "And none of them chose to be executed?")* Some of them did, and were executed. But most of them cooperated, and I therefore worked with them, transmitting coded messages. They did the transmitting and I monitored them for about a year or two, until it got to be an enormous organisation for all sorts of spies who had come here. They were transmitting back under our control to Germany, until, by the end of the war, we had every spy that had ever come here, had either been executed or was working for us.

(*NR: Do you remember anyone else you ran?*) "Well, I ran the man called Tate, who was a man called Wolf Schmitt. All these cases were written up in Sir John Masterman's book, and also by Nigel West".

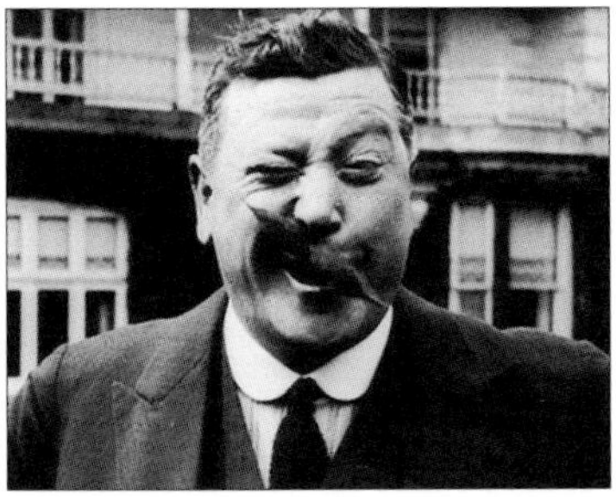
Harry Tate, the star of the music halls.

In a broadcast made soon after he landed, Wolf Schmidt reported to Hamburg that he had found lodgings in Barnet in Hertfordshire. Actually, he was now staying with Tar Robertson and his wife at Roundbush House, Radlett. He was to continue with his (supervised) broadcasting until May 1945. For most of that time, his wireless transmissions were supervised by Russell Lee, but sometimes by Ronnie Reed.

When Wolf Schmitt landed in England, he was carrying a passport in the name of Harry Williamson. But he was known to all as Harry. So he got his codename of *Tate*, because there was a music hall star called Harry Tate who did impressions of other people, and who looked like Williamson.

But then, "Harry Tate" was only the *stage* name of the performer. His real name was Ronald Hutchinson. But he wanted a more catchy name, so he took his name from the place of his first job, at Henry Tate and Sons (later Tate and Lyle) the sugar processors, and called himself Harry Tate. Though Harry Tate the music hall star is little remembered now, he had two catch-phrases which became popular. One was "Goodbyeee", which was turned into the popular song of the First World War. The other was an expression he used if there was an embarrassing gap in a conversation. For example, if someone was reluctant to refer to sex, they would say that a couple were having – er – "How's your father?" – to change the subject. Hence that expression!

He is also remembered in the expression "Harry Tate's Navy", which was the naval equivalent to the Home Guard. It was a collection of old civilian vessels with out of date equipment, manned by pensioners too old to serve in the regular navy. But that name arose because Harry Tate's persona portrayed a clumsy old dodderer who could never get the hang of new equipment. He is also the first known person to have had a personalised number-plate: it was T 8.

Wolf Schmitt *(Tate)* received instructions from Germany to visit Coventry in July 1941, and report on the extensive damage there. The devastation had been created on 14th November 1940, when the city was targeted by a massive air raid which killed 550 people and burnt out Coventry Cathedral. He went with Ronnie Reed, who helped him file the very detailed report, which Harry submitted to his masters in MI5 to see if they approved it. In fact, it would have given away far too much information to the Germans, so the final version sent was far less explicit than the original one. They also included some misleading information. For example, Harry reported that the GEC (General Electric Company), whose factory had been badly damaged, had moved to a new factory in Lanarkshire. This location was given, as we knew the Luftwaffe could not reach as far as Lanarkshire in Scotland, so the Germans would assume the GEC factory was now beyond their reach.

Prime Minister Churchill visiting the shell of Coventry Cathedral in September 1941, a couple of months after Reed and Tate visited the city.

After the War, Schmitt decided to keep his adopted name of Harry Williamson, and settled in Watford, where he became a leading breeder and judge of canaries. He died in 1992.

My father continues:

"Goester Caroli decided he didn't want to continue to cooperate, got out of the house, found a motor cycle and drove off to the east coast trying to get away by boat. But he didn't succeed, and eventually stayed in prison for the rest of the War." (*NR: "So he wasn't actually executed?"*) No, he wasn't. The people who were executed were some Dutchmen, who came to the coast in a boat and wouldn't cooperate at all. And there were one or two others who decided they still felt firmly that they wanted to help the Germans and couldn't help the British.

(*NR: "Did you ever come across an agent called Treasure?"*) Treasure was a woman who was – Yes – I met her, but I didn't have much to do with her, except to supervise her secret writing in invisible ink where she used to send letters back to Portugal.

Intellectuals in Hampstead

In August 1941 and 1942, my father was sent on training courses, at which he was assessed as possible officer material. The course was called the WOSB, pronounced "WAS-B": an acronym for War Office Selection Board. One of these courses took place at Catterick Camp. He remembered having to negotiate a course in a room where you had to try to get to the other side without touching the floor – a bit like the Krypton Factor. As another test, he and the others had to run, carrying large bales of straw along a field, without falling over. At any rate, we do know that by the end of the War he was promoted to Major.

Ronnie in January 1942, about the time he first met Mary.

Ronnie's QSL card, from his new address in Hampstead

By 1942, my father had moved out from living with his mother in Tufnell Park, and had rented a maisonette at 14b Belsize Lane, Hampstead. Mary Dyer (later my mother) was living at South Hill Park, looking out onto Hampstead Heath and the Hampstead Ponds.

But those with radical politics during the War had no real outlet for normal political thought and discussion. Throughout the War, the Government was a coalition of Conservative and Labour, fighting together to win the War. However, there was a small, radical, party one could join to discuss politics, and that was the Common Wealth Party, founded by JB Priestley in July 1942, but chaired by

Sir Harold Acland MP. My mother had to collect the subscriptions from the members in Belsize Ward, Hampstead, and indeed her collection book shows there were no less than 62 such members living in Belsize Ward. One of those she collected subs from was Ronnie Reed. Her collecting book gives Ronnie's new address at 14b Belsize Lane. They must have got chatting. He told her he was a radio engineer, and, as it happens, her radio was not working well (she said). So he came over to fix it. And that, according to Mary, is how they got together.

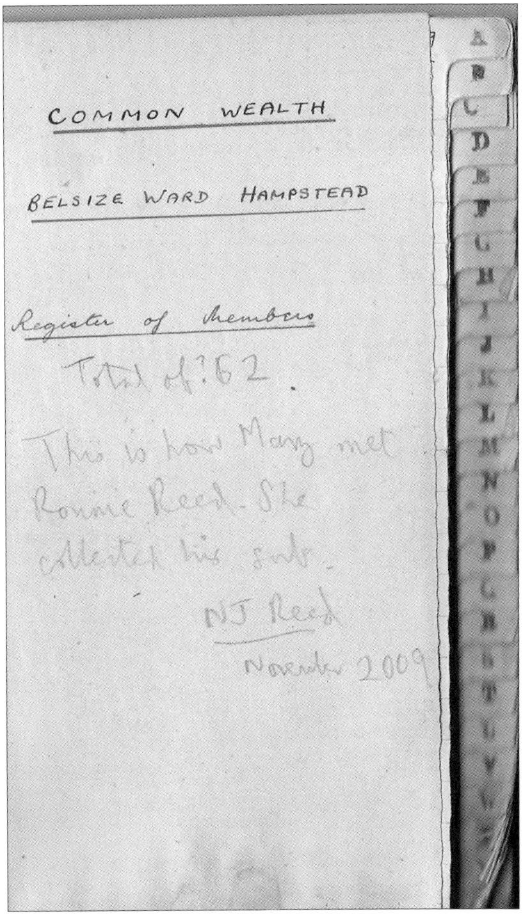

Mary Reed's Register of Members of the Common Wealth Party.

The entry for Ronald T Reed.

As young people, both my parents were quite left-wing and radical: indeed, later on, they became members of both South Place Ethical Society, and the Progressive League. My father said that in the 1930s he was a member of the Cremation Society, when that was a very radical idea, bitterly opposed by the churches. My parents shared left-wing politics, agnosticism, and a love of classical music. Such a combination

The Hampstead Ponds, with the houses in South Hill Park in the distance, where Mary Dyer was living.

is not very common, and these common interests must have drawn them together.

Indeed, it was a love of classical music which might very well have spelt the end to this budding romance. During the War, my mother was employed in doing technical drawings of electrical apparatus, and in the morning she would walk from South Hill Park down the hill, to catch her train at the end of the road. But while getting ready in the morning, she used to listen to Radio Hilversum, which was the best general radio station for classical music, apart from the BBC. Although it broadcast from Holland in Dutch, it could be easily heard in London. Without knowing Dutch, English listeners could normally pick out the name of the composer, and sometimes the piece itself. If my mother did not know the piece being played, she would almost always wait till the piece had ended, to find out the composer. She would then have to rush for the train, which she would sometimes catch, and sometimes not. If not, she would go for a walk around the

Hampstead Ponds, which were just up the road from the station, and then catch the next train.

One particular morning, she was listening to Radio Hilversum as usual, but became more and more intrigued as to its composer of the music being played. It went on for ages, but finally ended, and she found out who the composer was. She then looked at the clock, and realised there was no hope of her catching her usual train: she would have to catch the next one. So instead of walking round the Ponds, she got on with things at home before catching the next train. At the precise spot where she would have been walking, a landmine fell on the Ponds and killed everyone nearby. It would undoubtedly have killed her, had she been there. Ronnie was courting her at the time, knew her habits and then heard the news about the bomb. He actually rang up to check she was all right!

NINE

EDDIE CHAPMAN, ALIAS ZIGZAG

His first mission: to sabotage a factory

IN MY INTERVIEW, I specifically asked my father about Eddie Chapman, as I knew he had been his Case Officer. "Eddie Chapman: wonderful chap. He was in prison in the Channel Islands when the Germans invaded. They knew he was an expert on explosives, so they took him back into Germany, trained him, and dropped him, again, I think, in Cambridge and he came forward straight away to the British authorities and said, 'I have been trained to sabotage the De Havilland Factory at Hatfield, and I am very willing to help you do whatever you think.' So we agreed with him that we would camouflage a large part of the De Havilland Factory, to make it look as if they had blown up the transformers there. We arranged to get a message over, through one of the double agents, to say that this had been done. They sent over aircraft to photograph it, which we let through, and they saw the sabotage and said, 'Congratulations. Absolutely marvellous!' Then they said to him, 'We want you to come back, because we have a new and important task. But how will you get back to Germany?' He said to them, under our instructions, 'We'll find a way', and I took him up to Liverpool and got him a job on board a liner as a steward."

The archetypal photograph of a British policeman talking to a German officer during the German occupation of the Channel Islands.

Above are my father's recorded reminiscences of his dealings with Eddie, except for Sweden, to which we shall return. I first came across Chapman's name when the TV was about to show a film called *Triple Cross*, starring Christopher Plummer, which was released in 1967. It was probably in the early 1970s, when the family was at home in Dulwich, that my mother saw the trailer and said excitedly, "Look Ronnie. It's about Eddie Chapman." My father turned to her and said, "Mary, I have told you before. You are not supposed to discuss such matters in front of the boys." My mother looked rather embarrassed, and agreed she would not. I then asked, "Was he someone who Ronnie ran as

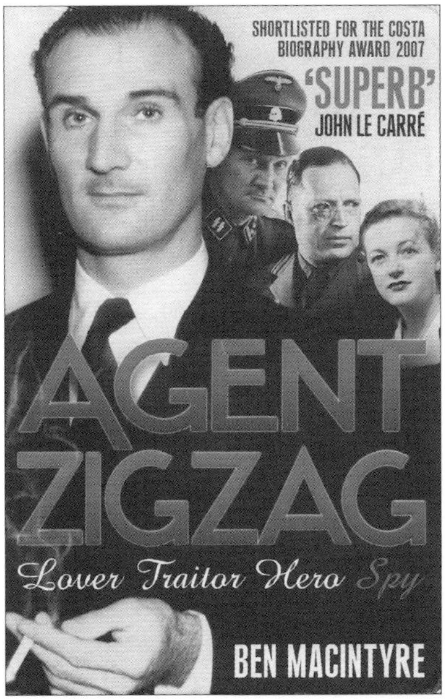

Agent Zigzag, by Ben Macintyre, and *Zigzag*, by Nicholas Booth.

an agent?" and my mother said, "Well, I think so", but would not be drawn any further. But we now know a great deal more about Eddie, and Ronnie's dealings with him.

Eddie Chapman's codename was Agent Zigzag. In 2007 two new books were published about him: *Agent Zigzag*, by Ben Macintyre, and *Zigzag*, by Nicholas Booth. Eddie himself published his memoirs in 1966.

My father was Zigzag's Case Officer from December 1942 to August 1944, and he was already in post when Eddie Chapman came on the scene.

Eddie in typical pose, beside his beloved Rolls Royce

Background

In the late 1930s, Eddie was a man-about-town with several girlfriends, and a liking for posh cars, such as the Rolls Royce shown on the previous page. When the War broke out, he was actually in prison in Jersey, having been caught blowing a safe in a night-club there. He was sentenced to their maximum of two years' hard labour for such an offence: a much lighter penalty than he would have faced in England. He was still inside when the Germans occupied the Channel Islands, and was only finally released in October 1941.

He and a fellow-prisoner called Faramus, then set up a hairdressing business in St Helier. But getting rapidly bored with that, they decided to write to the Governor to volunteer to join the German Secret Service. Eddie told him he hated the British Establishment, which, after all, kept on locking him up. The Germans listened to him politely, but took no further action. Two months later, he was at home when there was a hammering at the door. Two men, who turned out to be from the Gestapo, arrested him and Faramus, as possible members of the resistance. They were taken back to the port of St Malo on the mainland, then sent on by train to Paris, where they were charged with sabotage.

What had happened? Apparently, soon after they were released from prison in Jersey, several telephone wires on the island had been cut by the Resistance. The Nazis asked the local Jersey Police if they could suggest any suspects, and they immediately suggested those two jail-birds, Chapman and his friend! So for the first time, Chapman found himself being detained for a crime he had not done!

Training in France

He was kept in a prison on the east of Paris, at the Fort de Romainville. In December 1941, he was taken to the Commandant's Office, where he was interviewed by a senior officer about his professed wish to spy for the Germans. This was followed by two further interviews. Finally he was interviewed by a man who called himself Dr Graumann, and it was he who invited Eddie to work for them. He agreed.

Four months after his arrival in Paris, Eddy was taken to the Villa de la Bretonnière, in the country north-east of Nantes, a major port about halfway down the west coast of France. Then followed three months of training. He would need to have a Code Name, and they decided on the codename Fritz: they knew that, in the First World War, we had given the Germans the nick-name Fritz. In practice, in the Second World War, we tended to call Germans the Hun, which was much more descriptive of the way Hitler's Nazi thugs behaved.

A watchtower above the entrance to the Fort de Romainville, where Eddie was detained for four months.

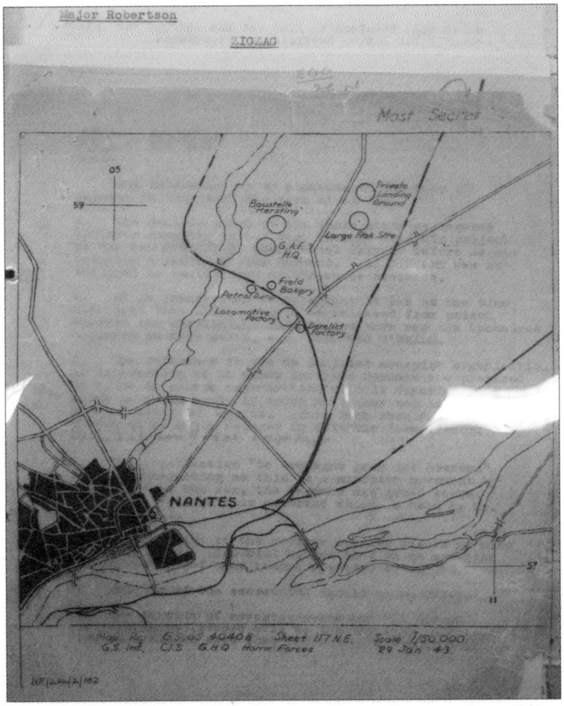

A contemporary map from the National Archives, showing military buildings NE of Nantes. These were presumably pinpointed by Eddie, but the Villa de la Bretonnière, where Eddie was trained, was close to the river at bottom right.

One of the many magnificent villas outside Nantes, whose grounds run down to the Erdre, a tributary of the Loire. It was in just such a villa that Eddie received three months of training to be a spy in England.

Previous German failures

The German Secret Service, known as the Abwehr, had tried sending secret agents to Britain before, but with little success. They normally sent Germans who were easily caught out once they started living in England. On one occasion, such an agent, formerly in the German army, got off a bus and immediately clicked his heels, as Nazi soldiers would do naturally at home. British soldiers do no such thing, so an observant passenger noted this, investigations took place, and the man was arrested. On another occasion, an agent in Britain, when asking the price of a railway ticket, was told it was "Ten and Six", meaning ten shillings and sixpence (about 50p). He handed over ten pounds and six shillings. The ticket seller called over the resident station policeman, and this agent too was arrested. At least Eddie, as an Englishman, was not going to make mistakes like that!

To England

Eventually, on 16th December 1942, Chapman took off in the plane bound for England. At the drop zone, when the signal was given Eddie jumped. Unfortunately, the hatch they had cut in the bottom of the plane was not large enough for his pack. So Eddie found himself underneath the plane in the howling wind, while his pack and parachute remained firmly stuck inside the plane. When he was suspended under the plane, it was a "very terrifying experience". Presumably, as well as having his breath sucked out of him, he had no idea whether they could get him free or whether they might have to land the plane with him still stuck face-down underneath it. One of his fellow-flyers had to give the pack a good kick to get it to go through the hatch, after which, he descended according to plan.

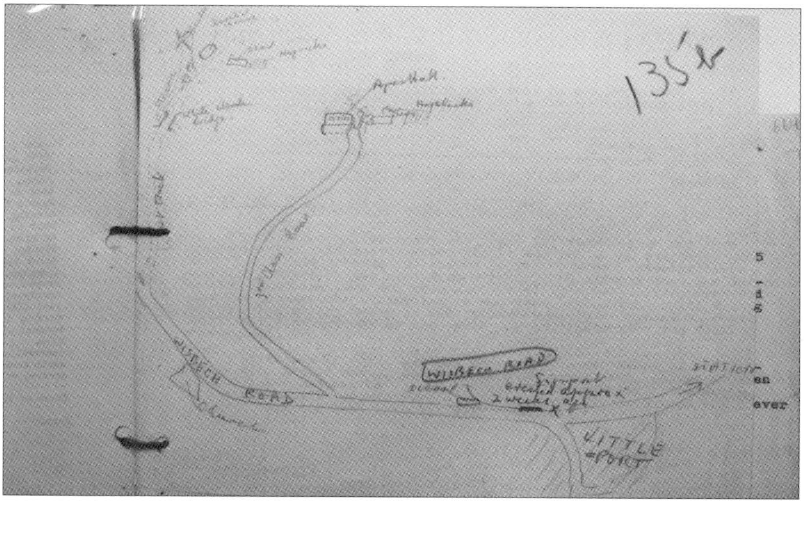

A contemporary sketchmap of Eddie's landing place at Apes Hall Farm, near Ely – from the National Archives.

The Royal Victoria Patriotic School in Wandsworth. It has now been converted into private flats, with a luxurious public restaurant underneath them.

The trouble was, it had taken so long to get his pack free that he landed twenty miles off target. He wandered about for about an hour. Then he found a farmhouse. It turned out to be Apes Hall Farm, near Ely. He knocked on the door and the farmer's wife let him in. She was not worried, because his first action was to ask if he could call the police. While they waited, she fed him tea and toast.

When the police arrived, they took him in a Black Maria from Norfolk down to the Royal Patriotic School in Wandsworth, which was used for the reception of enemy aliens. There he was officially detained. He was then put in another car and taken on a 30 minute drive to a large Victorian mansion: Camp 020 in Petersham, near Richmond. (It is still – in 2011 – a prison, now called Latchmere House, and is for remand prisoners.) There he was grilled by MI5 officers, and told them he must transmit that very evening, as that had been arranged with his German masters. But the British could not yet be sure of him, and would not allow this till they felt surer about him. After three days of interrogation by Colonel "Tin Eye" Stephens, Chapman, who was getting fed up being held in prison unable to do anything, sent a long letter to Colonel Stephens. This detailed all the ways in which he had tried to help the British with the extensive information he had picked up. But if he did not transmit back to Germany that evening, the Germans would get the firm impression that he had been captured.

Stephens then contacted the Double Cross team based at 58 St James's Street, which was headed by Sir John Masterman.

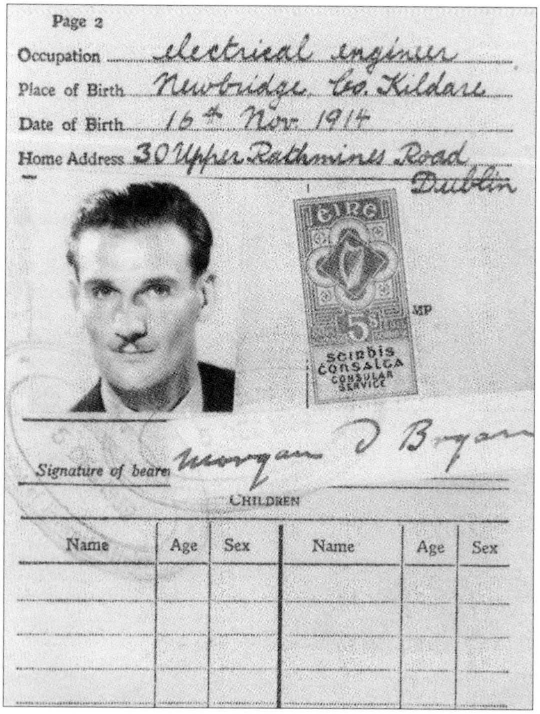
Page 2
Occupation electrical engineer
Place of Birth Newbridge Co. Kildare
Date of Birth 16th Nov. 1914
Home Address 30 Upper Rathmines Road Dublin

EIRE 5s SCIRBIS CONSALCA CONSULAR SERVICE

Signature of bearer Morgan D Bryan

CHILDREN

Name	Age	Sex	Name	Age	Sex

Chapman's fake Identity Card, with which he landed in England. It shows him as an Irishman called Morgan Bryan.

Stephens recommended that they "run" Chapman as a double agent, officially working for the Germans but in reality working for the British. This recommendation was accepted. However, Chapman would need an alias while working for the British. One agent had been called "Tate" because he looked like the comedian Harry Tate. Another was called Snow, which was almost an anagram of his real name Owens. A particularly ingenious agent, the Yugoslav Popov, liked variety in his private life. So his predilection for three-in-a-bed sex suggested his codename of "Tricycle". Chapman had already been zigzagging from Britain to Jersey, to France and now to Britain. What better name than "Zigzag"?

So it was Zigzag to whom Ronnie Reed was introduced in December 1942, once we had decided to use Eddie as a double-agent. And Ronnie explained to him that Eddie would have to live almost like a monk, cloistered in a cell, away from other members of the community. Eddie replied that after all the recent excitement he'd be quite glad of a quiet life, and, at first, he was.

The following day, Eddie sent his first coded message to his German controllers. They did not reply, but we knew they had received it. This was because of the most remarkable achievement the Allies attained, in the whole of the Second World War: the decipherment of German radio traffic sent in code.

The Victorian splendour of Bletchley Park, which is situated in Hertfordshire. Although this part was Victorian, much of the important decoding was carried out in huts scattered around the grounds.

The Decoding of Enigma

Down at Bletchley Park, we were receiving every coded message sent by the Germans, both from the armies in the field, and high-up communications between senior officers. More important, the mathematical genius Alan Turing had managed to devise the very first computers in the world, and build them at Bletchley. Coded messages were put into them, and as a result of a tiny flaw in the design of the German Enigma coding machines, it was possible to get a clue to the coding used. The new computers could test all the possibilities of decoding, using that tiny clue. As a result, messages were usually decoded within just a few hours, or sometimes, with good luck, in minutes. The decoders needed to be fast, because the Germans changed their codes every day to deal with the possibility of decoding. But in practice, that tiny flaw, and the power of the computer, allowed us to read the great majority of German messages. Churchill called these decoded messages his "golden geese that never cackled". They were golden, because of the information they contained, but never cackled, because our security was so tight that the Germans never had an inkling we were deciphering their codes.

Incidentally, not many people know why Apple Computers chose their name, and why the apple has a bite taken out of it. The fact is that Alan Turing was himself homosexual, when such conduct was still illegal. He had been caught with a young man by the police, and they said he was going to be prosecuted. He was such a private individual and so horrified at the prospect of a public trial, that he put poison in an apple and killed himself by eating it. Hence Apple Computers, as a tribute to the man who invented the electronic computer.

The Move to Hendon

Two Field Security Policemen, called Backwell and Tooth, were assigned to "mind" Eddie and take him to a safe house: 35 Crespigny Road, Hendon, north of Hampstead in NW London. There they were to act, not so much as his guards, but as minders, who could try to prevent him getting in trouble with the normal police, or bumping into his old associates unexpectedly. At the same time, they could be companions and even take him down to the local pub in the evening.

Shortly before Christmas 1942, the two men collected Eddie and his property from the prison at Camp 020. Eddie asked to borrow a pound to tip the sergeant who, he said, had looked after him so well. Only Chapman could have left the prison as though he had been checking out of a smart hotel. At 35 Crespigny Road, Ronnie Reed set up the radio room on the top floor, with an aerial at the back, while Chapman's bedroom was next door. Backwell asked him what type of literature he liked. Eddie told him Tennyson, German novels and French plays, the last two both in the original languages. A remarkable but genuine choice for a self-educated man, who could switch from such books to chatting about the best way to blow up a train. Every now and then he would regale his minders with tales, no doubt exaggerated but true, about some of his criminal escapades, which had up till then been unsolved crimes. They kept careful records of these confessions, just in case they became useful in the future…

Chapman's Creature Comforts

Soon after Chapman arrived at Crespigny Road, he asked for permission to see his former girlfriend Freda Stevenson, and her three-year-old daughter. He was the father of this child, but had never seen her. This set a problem. If Eddie met and became keen on both of them, that might make him reluctant to return to Germany. Ronnie stalled repeatedly, and Eddie became more and more difficult. Christmas was thus depressing for all of them.

Another problem emerged. Radio contact with Germany was very patchy: Eddie could receive transmissions from Germany, but could send nothing back. As they puzzled over this, Eddie mentioned to Ronnie that back in France, he had noticed a loose connection at the back of the wireless, and had mended it with a hot poker. Probably not the best way to improve transmission. Ronnie took the set home, got out his soldiering-iron and brought the set back. It worked perfectly, with no more patchy connections. On 27th December, 1942 Eddie transmitted again, and this time received an immediate acknowledgement. The game was on.

The Fairer Sex

This all helped to keep his mind off what was becoming very clear. He was becoming very sexually frustrated, and could not see why he should not be allowed any contact with Freda. My father put it like this. "He was a great womaniser. This presented us with a bit of a problem, which I eventually solved by taking him into a bar in Cork Street, giving him twenty pounds and saying, 'Take your pick! but be back in half an hour.' That's how that worked out alright. But Chapman was a remarkable, courageous, man who was a patriot and wanted to help the British authorities, but pretended to help the Germans. He wrote up his story eventually." (*NR: Yes – didn't you say he was sufficiently clever, being a cockney spiv, that he'd always got an answer when the Germans interrogated him?*) "Yes: always got an answer."

(*NR: "Wasn't there an incident when you said he had to broadcast at a particular time and he was busy with a girlfriend?"*)

"That was very difficult, yes. He was living in a house in Crespigny Road, Hendon, and he'd got to transmit at 9 o'clock that night, but he was dying to see an ex-girlfriend of his, who we brought up for him. So at 7 o'clock that evening, I said, 'Eddie: we're on the air at 9 o'clock. Don't forget.' At 8 o'clock, I went back up to the bedroom and said, 'You've got an hour, Eddie.' and at a quarter to nine I banged on the door and said, 'You've only got 15 minutes, Eddie.' and he came to the door, and said. 'Oh no, not just 15 minutes.' I said, 'It's time to go on the air.' Eventually we did".

By January 1943, Eddie was insisting he would not stay any longer unless matters changed. He now started asking about Betty Farmer, whom he last seen in 1939 in Jersey. He then became more and more

Ronnie operating a captured German wireless transmitter out in a field somewhere.

insistent that he must see Freda Stevenson and his daughter by her. Finally, at the end of January, it was decided to trust Freda. On 26th January, she was brought up to the Brent Bridge Hotel, where Eddie and his minders joined them. While Eddie and Freda got reacquainted upstairs, his minders looked after the daughter Diane. Eddie told Freda that he had escaped from Jersey, all charges had been dropped, and he was expecting to be called up for the army. She asked no further questions and meanwhile, moved into 35 Crespigny Road.

The fact that she did not ask many questions can be explained by the situation before the war. At that time, Eddie had various male friends who preferred to remain in the shadows, and not be overheard when discussing 'business'. In the middle of the war, nothing had really changed. The only difference might have been if one of Eddie's minders told her he was engaged in important war work. Which she could either believe or not, as she chose.

The important thing was the result. Eddie was now quite happy living with Freda and Diane, and showed no inclination to chat up other women or renew his acquaintance with his old haunts. He settled down to a form of married life: he actually got engaged to Freda, and his black moods vanished. Perhaps the only difference was that, when Freda was not around, he tapped out his messages back to Germany. Meanwhile, his masters in Britain knew that he was now highly unlikely to defect to the Germans, even if he went back there. He had too much private life invested back in England.

Inside the Mosquito factory at Hatfield.

The Aircraft Factory at Hatfield

Now came the great test. Eddie's mission was to blow up the De Havilland factory in Hatfield, some fifteen miles north of Hendon. This was producing the Mosquito airplane. It is little remembered now, but these planes had become very important and effective bombers ever since their invention in 1940. Constructed almost entirely out of wood, each plane could carry 4000 tons of high explosive as far as Berlin which, by 1943, they had started to reach. And with a top speed of 400 mph, they could normally outrun any German fighters. Goering, in charge of the Luftwaffe, was infuriated by them. "It makes me furious when I see the Mosquito. The British, who can afford aluminium better than we can, knock together a beautiful wooden aircraft, and give it a speed which they have increased yet again. There is nothing the British do not have. They have the geniuses and we have the nincompoops. After the war is over I'm going to buy a British radio set. Then at least I shall own something that has always worked!"

Blowing up the Mosquito factory at Hatfield could have had a major effect on the British war effort. If Eddie had really been going to carry out his mission to bomb the de Havilland Factory, he would need to reconnoitre. Even if we were going to simulate an explosion, he would still need to know everything he would have seen, so he could tell a plausible story when he got back to Germany. So they made various trips around Hatfield, first of all to look at the factory. Eddie's minder Backwell stood with his back to the factory while Eddie told him everything he could see.

At lunch they adjourned to the Comet public house beside the factory, and compared notes. On another occasion they went back to the site of Eddie's landing near Ely, and then took the train to London, as he would tell his controllers he had done. Everything he should have observed he would have to observe, to make his story plausible. They also started calling in at the Hendon Way pub, so Eddie could talk knowledgeably about his 'local'.

Bring in the magician!

But if Eddie was to get the Germans to think he had accomplished his mission, the British needed to give them evidence they would believe. They would have to disguise the factory to make it look as though it had been damaged. This was where they brought in Sir John Turner, the resident camouflage expert in Britain.

Deceiving Rommel

Out in the western desert in Africa in 1942, they had called in the services of Jasper Maskelyne, the most famous British magician of his day. In the 1930s he filled theatres in the West End with his shows. Eventually his unit had a whole team of varied talents working on deception. One of the biggest tasks was building dummy aircraft, or even, on at least one occasion, a whole dummy airfield full of dummy aircraft. The Germans were not always fooled. On one occasion, a German bomber flew low over one of our dummy airfields and dropped a bomb. It was made of wood!

Jasper Maskelyne celebrating after winning a bet. A hotel proprietor had seen him on stage, escaping from a locked coffin. The proprietor bet him he could not do the same trick with a coffin on the bar of his hotel in Bayswater. Jasper won the bet: in twenty seconds! Here he is celebrating his win.

Maskelyne and his team had been busy deceiving Rommel in Africa, before El Alamein. Our counter-attack against the Germans was going to come from the north. So we thought we'd try to persuade him we would be attacking from the south. Maskelyne and his friends erected a dummy army of over 2000 tanks, as well as a fake pipeline for water to supply the fake army. It was easily visible from the air, and from the air seemed to be only half complete. Its slow progress appeared to indicate there could be no attack before November, so Rommel went home on leave. Our attack, marking the start of the Battle of El Alamein, began on 23rd October 1942, and caught Rommel napping!

Field Marshall Rommel, wearing the Iron Cross, Germany's highest decoration for soldiers.

Rommel's reputation has never been higher than now, with historians applauding his outstanding abilities as a commander. He was indeed brilliant as a tactician, but one has to remember this was not the only occasion when his timing was woefully wrong. On the other occasion, he took a decision without any misinformation from us. This was just before D-day, when Rommel was in charge of the whole Western front and the counter-measures to D-Day. In June 1944 everyone knew the invasion was imminent. Rommel had told his side that that battle, against our Invasion, must be won on the beaches: to throw us back into the sea. But the weather experts told Rommel the weather was so bad, they said the British could not possibly launch the invasion of

France until the weather improved. So he left France and went back to Germany for his wife's birthday – which happened to be D-day – the 6th of June.

In our case, despite the atrocious weather, we found it almost imperative to invade in June, or the invasion could be delayed for months. Also, the location of our invasion was only too likely to be revealed after such a long delay. In fact, our weather men found a slight "window of opportunity" on 6th June, and led us to take that chance. It thus turned out that, on the two most important dates in his entire career – when his presence on the spot was vitally important – Rommel was on leave in Germany.

The factory "explosion"

Back to Eddie's mission, to blow up the Mosquito factory at Hatfield. We would have to make it look as though he had succeeded. So the camouflage experts built four replica transformers out of wood, painted grey to look like metal. Two of these would be placed on their sides, to make it seem they had been blown over. At the same time, the real transformers would be covered with netting so that, from the air, it would seem there was simply a large hole in the ground where they had stood. Other brick walls were draped with canvas, to make it look as though they had been half demolished by the explosion. Any German plane flying over would be completely convinced. The night of 31st January 1943 was chosen for the event, when the camouflage experts would have three hours of complete darkness before the moon rose.

The two doors seem to have been blown outward by the force of the explosion. The two "transformers" lie at an angle on the ground, as if blown out of position. They were made of wood, while the real electrical transformers were safe inside the camouflage netting.

"Fixing" the newspaper reports

If the deception plan was to succeed, they wanted something to appear in the national press afterwards. Masterman went to see the Editor of The Times. He explained what was planned, and how they would like a small paragraph to appear, referring to the "explosion". But the Editor had firm opinions. The Times was a newspaper of record. Nothing could appear in the paper which the Editor knew to be untrue. Some other paper might be willing to fall in with their plans, but The Times could not allow it.

Masterman then tried the Daily Express, and found their principles far more flexible. If it helped the war effort, that was fine! But their Editor pointed out a problem. If he were to try to publish anything which could lead to a lowering of morale, like this report, the censor would strike it out. They agreed on a compromise. A short report would appear, but only in the earliest editions. That way, it could appear that the censor had had it removed from the paper, once he had seen it.

The plan succeeds

On 31st January 1943, everything went as planned. The camouflage was erected, and the following morning a brief paragraph appeared in early editions of the Express. This reported "an explosion in a factory in the outskirts of London." My father wrote a report the day after the "explosion".

This picture from the National Archives shows the Mosquito factory at Hatfield from the air. This is taken from high up, and has a rectangle in black ink marked on it. The rectangle is so small that one cannot make out anything inside the lines, even with a magnifying glass. My father's report says he was arranging for aerial photos taken for the British experts to see if their work was likely to mislead the Germans.

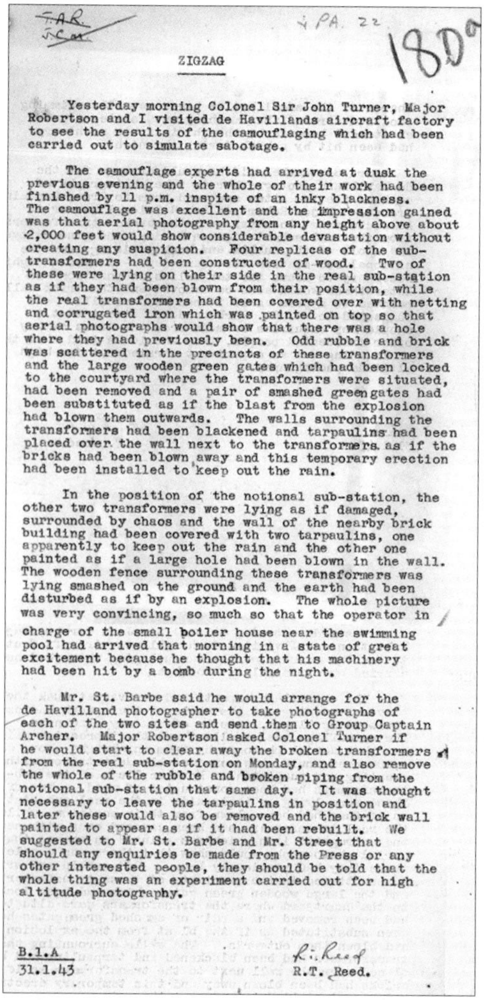

T.A.R.
J.C.M.
PA. 22
180a

ZIGZAG

Yesterday morning Colonel Sir John Turner, Major Robertson and I visited de Havillands aircraft factory to see the results of the camouflaging which had been carried out to simulate sabotage.

The camouflage experts had arrived at dusk the previous evening and the whole of their work had been finished by 11 p.m. inspite of an inky blackness. The camouflage was excellent and the impression gained was that aerial photography from any height above about 2,000 feet would show considerable devastation without creating any suspicion. Four replicas of the sub-transformers had been constructed of wood. Two of these were lying on their side in the real sub-station as if they had been blown from their position, while the real transformers had been covered over with netting and corrugated iron which was painted on top so that aerial photographs would show that there was a hole where they had previously been. Odd rubble and brick was scattered in the precincts of these transformers and the large wooden green gates which had been locked to the courtyard where the transformers were situated, had been removed and a pair of smashed green gates had been substituted as if the blast from the explosion had blown them outwards. The walls surrounding the transformers had been blackened and tarpaulins had been placed over the wall next to the transformers as if the bricks had been blown away and this temporary erection had been installed to keep out the rain.

In the position of the notional sub-station, the other two transformers were lying as if damaged, surrounded by chaos and the wall of the nearby brick building had been covered with two tarpaulins, one apparently to keep out the rain and the other one painted as if a large hole had been blown in the wall. The wooden fence surrounding these transformers was lying smashed on the ground and the earth had been disturbed as if by an explosion. The whole picture was very convincing, so much so that the operator in charge of the small boiler house near the swimming pool had arrived that morning in a state of great excitement because he thought that his machinery had been hit by a bomb during the night.

Mr. St. Barbe said he would arrange for the de Havilland photographer to take photographs of each of the two sites and send them to Group Captain Archer. Major Robertson asked Colonel Turner if he would start to clear away the broken transformers from the real sub-station on Monday, and also remove the whole of the rubble and broken piping from the notional sub-station that same day. It was thought necessary to leave the tarpaulins in position and later these would also be removed and the brick wall painted to appear as if it had been rebuilt. We suggested to Mr. St. Barbe and Mr. Street that should any enquiries be made from the Press or any other interested people, they should be told that the whole thing was an experiment carried out for high altitude photography.

B.1.A
31.1.43

R. Reed
R.T. Reed.

And here is my father's report, from the National Archives. Note the initials, at top left, which show it was to be seen by Tar Robertson, and by J.C.M(asterman).

Meantime, Eddy reported by radio that "Walter" (the code name for the factory) had been "blown in two places." Graumann broke open the champagne at the Villa in France. And indeed, when the Germans sent over a plane to look for the evidence, we carefully let it through and back to Germany, carrying with it the photos with the "proof". So there must be a photo taken by the German aircraft which we let through to photograph the "success". This photo must be buried somewhere in the German archives.

TEN

CHAPMAN'S SECOND MISSION

To blow up a ship

NOW WAS the time for Eddie to return to occupied Europe and carry out some extensive spying for the British. He was to find out everything he could about the German Abwehr: the counter-espionage section of their Army. But the Germans would not play ball. They were keen to keep their "top agent" in England, where he could do important spying for them. So when he requested a submarine to pick him up, they just replied that that was impossible.

Engineering Eddie's return

It now seemed the best way to get him back to the Continent would be to make it appear that Eddie was now in trouble, and needed to be brought back. His supposed friend, Jimmy Hunt, would have to be "put out of action". The real Jimmy Hunt was actually in prison, but the Germans did not know that. While broadcasting back to Germany, Eddie suddenly broke off his transmission and tapped "PPPPP", the agreed signal for Danger. The Germans completely ignored it! My father was furious. They would have to make it obvious. So the next day they transmitted, "Dangerous to continue transmitting. Things getting awkward. Essential to come back with Jimmy." When back in Germany, Eddie would explain that Jimmy thought he might not be paid, and insisted on coming too. He had got suspicious when the Germans refused to send the submarine, and they had broadcast "PPPPP" when Jimmy had seen a police car in the street outside. We then planted a couple of newspaper stories saying a man had been arrested in connection with enquiries to do with gelignite.

Meantime, Eddie broadcast back, "Jimmy arrested. Closing transmitter. Will try to get back to Lisbon."

By saying this, he convinced them he was in danger, and that they should bring back their prized agent.

When he went back, there was always a danger he would be caught out. So it was vital he did not know about Enigma, and the fact that we had broken German codes. My father therefore told him it was far too difficult to try to keep tabs on possible spies, and that the German codes were so complex it really was impossible to break them. As the Germans themselves had said that, Eddie was convinced it was true.

Eddie now had to part from Freda and his daughter. But their relationship had worked in our favour: since he was very keen on family life, and had been living a contented family life for several months, that gave him a major incentive to continue supporting the Allies, and want to come back to Britain once it was possible. So after three months of domestic bliss, the house at Crespigny Road was closed down. Eddie was on his way.

How the Adelphi advertised itself, probably in the 1920s.

Liverpool to Lisbon

Chapman travelled up to Liverpool with Ronnie and Allan Tooth, one of his minders. Chapman and Tooth stayed at the Washington Hotel, while Ronnie stayed at the Adelphi, which was rather grander, and is now an icon of art deco. Ronnie used a local MI5 man to steal a set of seaman's papers from the Liverpool Shipping office. He then filled them out in the name of Hugh Anson, in a corner of the Flying Dutchman pub, down by the docks.

Eddie was going to be returned to Germany by way of Lisbon, a neutral country. But he would leave from Liverpool aboard a coal steamer, the City of Lancaster. Its captain was summoned to the shipping office to meet my father, now Major Ronald Reed. He explained that he worked for intelligence, and that the Captain would be taking on board an assistant steward, called Hugh Anson. Ronnie explained that "Hugh" was actually a double agent, doing vital work, and that he would jump ship while they were in Lisbon. His cover story would be that he was a habitual criminal who had been released early from jail on condition that he joined the Navy.

The very grand dining-room of the Adelphi Hotel.

A bedroom and bathroom in the Adelphi. Ronnie's rooms must have been much like this.

In other words, he was being given the chance to turn over a new leaf. When he jumped ship at Lisbon, it would simply be assumed that he had turned over an old leaf instead, and was back to his old tricks.

To contact Eddie abroad, Ronnie arranged with him that he would use the Times personal column. Reed would say, "Mrs West thanks the anonymous donor for the gift of £46." The last digit, 6, meant that our side had picked up Eddie's message no 6. The name of the fictional Mrs West actually came from their cleaning lady at Crespigny Road. Finally, they laid an "elephant trap". While he was in Germany, if any further German agents were going to be sent over, Eddie was to give them a phone number, so they could contact his friend and collaborator Jimmy Hunt. In fact, the phone rang straight into my father's office, so he could make appropriate arrangements to pick them up immediately. Meantime, Bletchley Park were warned to look out for any transmission from Fritz, his German code name.

The City of Lancaster, on which Eddie sailed to Lisbon.

In the early evening, Ronnie and Allan Tooth followed Eddie, at a discreet distance, down to the docks to join his ship. They lost him, or rather, he gave them the slip. They finally returned to Ronnie's hotel, the Adelphi. On an impulse, my father rang the Washington Hotel, and found that Eddie had been at the bar, chatting up a prostitute. He said he did not wish to join them for dinner, as he was "busy". They agreed to meet at Ronnie's rooms in the Adelphi. After dinner there, the two went up to Ronnie's room. There, they found Eddie already in Ronnie's room. As my father later reported, "Zigzag had, in some way, managed to obtain entry, and was reclining on the bed awaiting dinner, which he had ordered on my telephone, together with a number of bottles of beer." It turned out later he had also stolen my father's gold-plated scissors and nail file. As one of his earlier colleagues had reported, Eddie would do his duty for his country, but would also be picking your pocket at the same time.

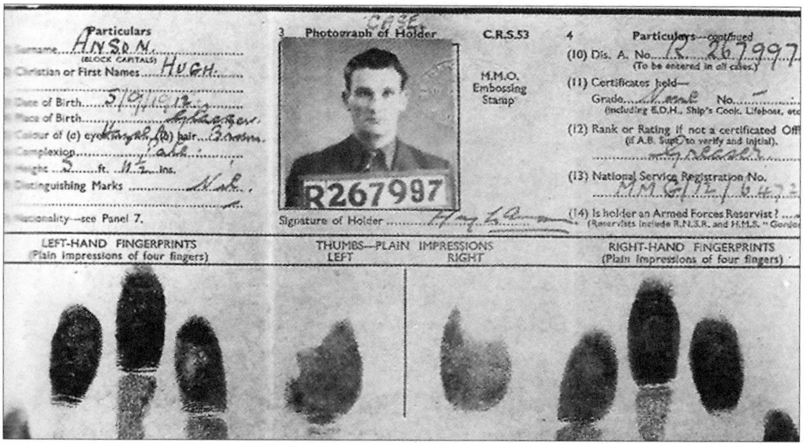
Particulars
(BLOCK CAPITALS)
Christian or First Names
Date of Birth
Place of Birth
Colour of (a) eyes (b) hair
Complexion
Height ... ft. ... ins.
Distinguishing Marks
Nationality—see Panel 7.
3 Photograph of Holder
C.R.S.53
M.M.O. Embossing Stamp
R267997
Signature of Holder
4 Particulars—continued
(10) Dis. A. No. (To be entered in all cases.)
(11) Certificates held—
Grade ... No. ... (including E.D.H., Ship's Cook, Lifeboat, etc)
(12) Rank or Rating if not a certificated Off (if A.B. Supt. to verify and initial).
(13) National Service Registration No.
(14) Is holder an Armed Forces Reservist? (Reservists include R.N.S.R. and H.M.S. "Gordo
LEFT-HAND FINGERPRINTS (Plain impressions of four fingers)
THUMBS—PLAIN IMPRESSIONS LEFT RIGHT
RIGHT-HAND FINGERPRINTS (Plain impressions of four fingers)

Chapman's fake identity documents, filled out in the name of Hugh Anson.

Just after Eddie set sail, my father made a detailed report on the agent he had been running for the last eight weeks. "Zigzag is himself a most absorbing person. Reckless and impetuous, moody and sentimental, he becomes on acquaintance an extraordinarily likeable character." He was to find out more about his character when Eddie arrived in Lisbon.

After leaving the ship in Lisbon, Eddie joined four of his companions in the British Seamen's Institute, where they all proceeded to get drunk. After a time, he said he was off to see a friend. In fact, he went to the pre-arranged address where he could make contact with his German masters. When he got there, he gave the password "Joli Albert", but it was clear that no-one recognised it. Unknown to him, this safe address had been vacated by the Germans, and ordinary civilians were there. But we had no way of telling him this once he was in Lisbon.

Chapman realised he was getting nowhere, so he left the "safe" house and found his way to "George's", a brothel-bar beside the docks. For his return journey from England, Chapman had been supplied with fake identity documents, in the name of Hugh Anson, describing him as an assistant steward. In George's, Eddie chatted up a lady of the night called Anita. Little did he know that in her spare time, Anita worked for MI6. She later reported that Eddie had told her, in strictest confidence, that his real name was Reed! Nothing like stirring things up a bit. And no doubt he stirred things up with Anita that night.

One of the pieces of explosive coal which Eddie took on board *The City of Lancaster*.

The next day Eddie went directly to the German Legation and underwent another interview. Eddie explained to them that when he was being trained in Berlin, he was taught how to construct a bomb inside a piece of coal. It would remain inert if placed inside a ship's locker. But when shovelled into the stoke-hole, it would explode and sink the ship. Eddie was offering to use such a bomb on his own ship. His interviewer reported this offer to his superiors in Berlin. The message was intercepted and decoded at Bletchley Park. So it was through this source that Tar Robertson heard of Chapman's offer. He was horrified at it, with Eddie offering to blow up a British ship in a neutral port. My father could not believe that Eddie had turned traitor so quickly. But it was vitally important that Eddie did not destroy the ship, thus violating Portuguese neutrality and breaking the Geneva Convention at the same time. According to my father, MI6 sent their man out there, Ralph Jarvis, to see Chapman. Jarvis introduced himself to Eddie, and then said, "It is vitally important you do not blow up that bomb." Eddie replied, "I don't know what you are talking about." And when Jarvis repeated his remarks, he got the same reply.

Back in London, we remembered that, when we sent Eddie back to German-occupied territory, we warned him to be extremely careful. The Germans would be highly suspicious of him, and just one slip could prove fatal. Eddie did not know Jarvis, and if Jarvis had actually been a German agent, Eddie's acceptance of his instruction would have immediately told the Germans he was working for us. Hence his non-committal reply. The only thing we could now do, was to send someone he knew, to see him. Someone like my father. So Ronnie was flown out to Lisbon.

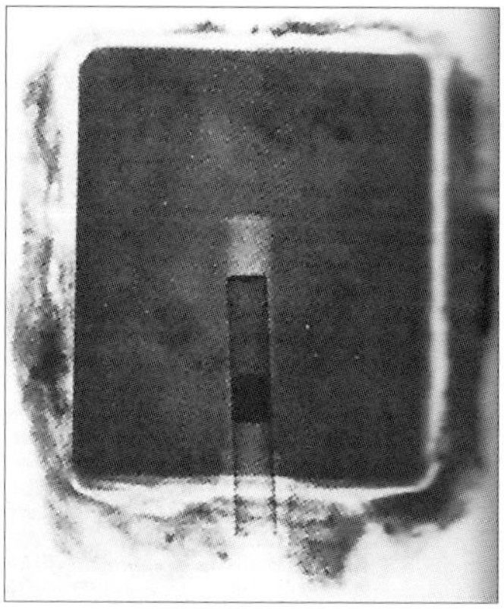

An X-ray of the coal, showing the explosive charge inside it.

Meanwhile, still in Lisbon, Eddie was given the bomb he had asked for, sent to him from Berlin. He had given the Germans a sample from his ship's (Welsh) coal. They had made what looked like an exact copy of it. But in fact they had taken two pieces of explosive, moulded them to the right shape, and then sprinkled coal dust on the outside. Eddie now returned to Anita's flat, with these two pieces of explosive coal in his rucksack.

Finally my father arrived in Lisbon, on 23rd March 1943, and went to see Eddie. As he walked in the door, Eddie said, "Ronnie! Am I glad to see you! I've had this man Jarvis on my back telling me what to do. But I didn't know him from Adam, and wasn't going to admit anything to him." My father replied, "Eddie: you must not blow up that bomb. It could seriously endanger the war effort." Eddie replied, "That's fine: I never intended to use it." It turned out that, back in Britain, Rothschild had said he would be very pleased if Chapman could obtain samples of some of the German sabotage devices. This coal was just the sort of thing he wanted to see, which was why Eddie intended to bring it back to England.

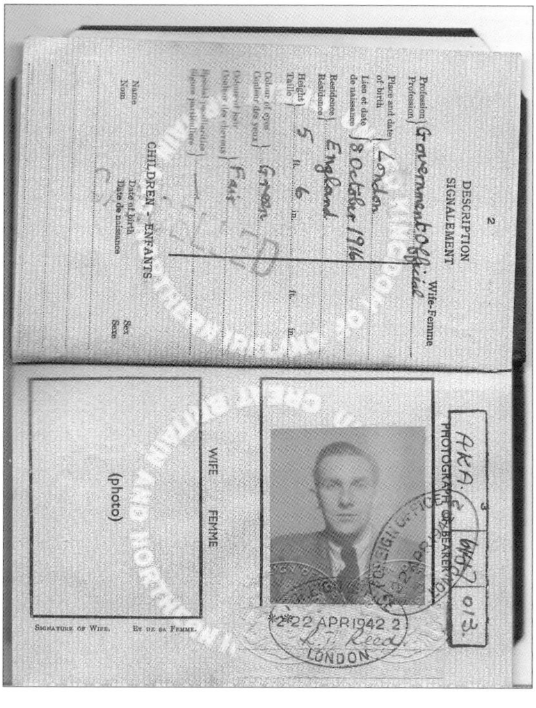

The passport on which Ronnie travelled to Lisbon. Note that he has no moustache at that time. This may have deliberately made him less recognisable.

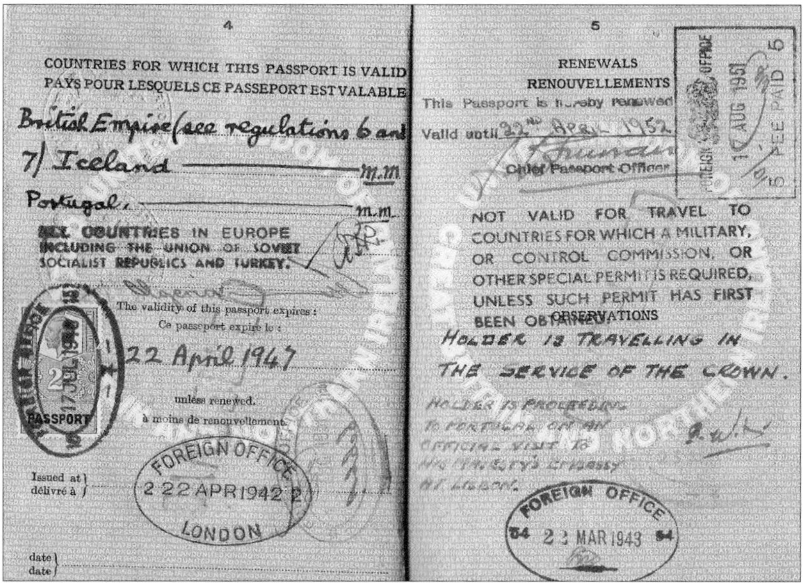
4

COUNTRIES FOR WHICH THIS PASSPORT IS VALID
PAYS POUR LESQUELS CE PASSEPORT EST VALABLE

British Empire (see regulations 6 and 7) Iceland m.m.
Portugal m.m.

EXC. COUNTRIES IN EUROPE INCLUDING THE UNION OF SOVIET SOCIALIST REPUBLICS AND TURKEY.

The validity of this passport expires:
Ce passeport expire le:
22 April 1947
unless renewed.
à moins de renouvellement.

PASSPORT
17 JUL 1946

Issued at / délivré à
FOREIGN OFFICE
22 APR 1942
LONDON

date / date

5

RENEWALS
RENOUVELLEMENTS
This Passport is hereby renewed
Valid until 22nd April 1952
Chief Passport Officer

FOREIGN OFFICE
1 AUG 1951
FEE PAID 5

NOT VALID FOR TRAVEL TO COUNTRIES FOR WHICH A MILITARY, OR CONTROL COMMISSION, OR OTHER SPECIAL PERMIT IS REQUIRED, UNLESS SUCH PERMIT HAS FIRST BEEN OBTAINED

OBSERVATIONS
HOLDER IS TRAVELLING IN THE SERVICE OF THE CROWN.
HOLDER IS PROCEEDING TO PORTUGAL ON AN OFFICIAL VISIT TO HIS MAJESTY'S EMBASSY AT LISBON.

FOREIGN OFFICE
23 MAR 1943

The page of Ronnie's passport, issued in April 1942. It says (bottom right), "Holder is proceeding to Portugal on an official visit to His Majesty's Embassy at Lisbon." Next to this is a Foreign Office stamp dated 22nd March 1943.

"Anyway," said Eddie, "I don't want this piece of explosive coal. Here you are: you take it." Ronnie replied, "Not bloody likely! You can take it back on board the ship, and the captain can deal with it." So that's what eventually happened.

Zigzag was now flown from Lisbon to Madrid. Over the next five days, he was interrogated by several different members of the Abwehr. He wanted to meet his former boss and friend Dr Graumann, but was told he had been sent to the East. After ten days, Eddie was put on a train for Berlin. There, after another day of interrogation, he was told he was going to Norway.

However, after this length of time, the Germans were more suspicious of him, because the bombs Eddie had said he would place on the ship, had not in fact gone off. So finally, the British launched Operation Damp Squib. When the boat finally got back to Britain, to Glasgow, a group of special police came on board and started searching through the coal bunkers, then started throwing the coal out, piece by piece, over the side. It was observed, and reported, that every time they did this, they ducked. Finally, after some hours, an officer covered in coal dust emerged from the bunkers, clutching what looked like a piece of coal. The entire crew were then interrogated about the outward voyage, and what they remembered about Assistant Steward Hugh Anson (Eddie's new identity). They were then sworn to secrecy. Needless to say, all this swept through the docks of Glasgow, and beyond. It even reached the ears of the German High Command, and was enough to convince them that Eddie had indeed tried to blow up the ship, as he said he would.

ELEVEN

CHAPMAN'S THIRD MISSION

To monitor the German rockets

AFTER MY FATHER'S last encounter with Eddie, British Intelligence lost sight of Eddie for months. It turned out he had been sent to Oslo in Norway. Dr Graumann had been brought back from the Eastern Front and was waiting for him at Oslo Airport. Graumann interrogated Eddie once again, but this time, it seemed he was keen for Eddie to give the "right" answers. If Eddie came through the test, then his mentor would have reason to be proud of him, and Graumann would not be sent back to the Eastern Front. Eddie was installed in a hotel in Oslo taken over by the German Army of Occupation, while being interrogated by Graumann. During this time, Eddie found out what it was like to be despised by the free people of Norway.

Quisling (*left*) sitting next to Himmler and other friends. The word "quisling" has now entered many languages, meaning a traitor to one's country.

Norway's puppet government was led by Vidkun Quisling. But the Norwegians had become quite skilled at making known their displeasure of the Nazis. For example, waiters in restaurants would always serve Norwegians first. In buses, no-one would sit beside a German: even if the bus was jam-packed, the seat beside a German was always empty! Eventually, the Germans passed a law to make it illegal to stand on a bus, if there was a vacant seat!

After Dr Graumann had interviewed Chapman for two weeks, he took his detailed report to Berlin. There, his bosses still could not make up their minds, and for five days discussed: Was Chapman a British stooge? Was he a romancer who just invented what they wanted to hear? On the other side, there was plenty of evidence to back up Chapman's account, including reports in the British press.

Finally Graumann returned to Oslo. He announced that the Abwehr had accepted Chapman's account, and were awarding him a sum equivalent to £4 million in modern money: three quarters of what was agreed in his original contract. Double agents did not normally quibble about their financial rewards: but Eddie did! He accepted it, grudgingly. It was going to be placed in a bank account, for him to draw on "when necessary". While he stayed in Norway, he would also receive a monthly salary of 400 Kroner, or about £2000 a month, in modern terms. What he did not yet know was that, if he asked for a large sum, say, towards buying a yacht, Graumann would get the money, but only handed over half of it. The rest, Graumann would keep for himself. So Eddie's salary enriched both him and his boss. At one point in his interview, my father talked briefly of Eddie's time in "Sweden" – though, as we have seen, it was actually Norway, another Scandinavian country. According to Ronnie, "He had a wonderful time when he was training in Sweden. They gave him a yacht and lots of blond Swedish women, and he came back here, roaring like a lion."

The Iron Cross, which Graumann presented to Chapman, next to its black case.

After Graumann came back to tell Chapman that his story had been accepted, Chapman signed the receipt for his reward: primarily, for supposedly blowing up the Mosquito factory. Graumann then got solemnly to his feet, and handed him a small black leather case. Inside was an Iron Cross: the Germans' highest decoration for bravery. It was awarded for his "outstanding zeal and success". No other British agent ever won the Iron Cross – and it was won by an agent working for us! No wonder MI5 now regard that Cross as the pinnacle of their achievement during the Second World War.

Misdirecting the Doodle-bugs

My father's recorded interview only speaks briefly about Eddie's later career. That's why Ronnie kicked himself later for not mentioning to me his own special mission, flying out to see Eddie in Lisbon. He told me about it verbally. In the recorded interview, my father just says, "Eddie went back to Lisbon, and then through to Germany, and was retrained, and eventually flew back to this country, came down again in Cambridge, and rang me up at night and said, 'It's Eddie. I'm back, with a new task.' He worked here for a year or so after that, but he was a very erratic character."

On the day he landed, 28th June 1944, he was taken to Camp 020 at Petersham, as before. There he was questioned for an hour, before it became clear he was simply too tired to be debriefed further. He slept overnight at a house in Hill Street, Mayfair.

The Naval and Military Club, commonly known as the "In and Out" Club, because of the prominent words on the gateways at the entrance (and exit). It looked like this until 1999, when it moved out to St James's.

The following morning, he was given a substantial breakfast at the Naval and Military Club at 94 Piccadilly. His hosts were Tar Robertson and his Case Officer Ronnie Reed. This time his British training really showed. He had came back with a vast knowledge of the German secret service, possible targets, important buildings: even a roll of film with photos of senior Abwehr officers.

What, then, was Eddie's "new task", for which the Germans had prepared him? He landed, in fact, just three weeks after D-Day, which was the 6th of June 1944. But one week after D-Day, the first of Hitler's terrible new weapons: the V-1, commonly known as the doodle-bug, was launched on Britain. These were pilotless flying bombs, each of which, when their fuel ran out, dropped nearly 2000 lbs of explosive

A V-1 Rocket, or "doodlebug".

on or near London. On 15th June, over 200 of them landed in Britain, 45 on London itself. Overall, they tended to land slightly short of central London, which was their target. However, the Germans had no way of knowing whether they were reaching their targets or not. The only way to find out was to ask their agents in Britain, of which they thought they had several. (Of course, they did not realise that every agent they landed had been captured, and most of them "turned".)

So if the Germans wanted to know where their bombs were dropping, we decided to try to make their aim even more unreliable, and get the agents to report that most bombs were landing north and west of central London. Since the bombs were already landing short, i.e. south and east of London, it was hoped to increase that error, and thus reduce the devastation affecting Westminster, and the important offices based around the seat of government. It was decided, in fact, to try to shift their target towards a notional target of North Dulwich Station in SE London. (This, as it happens, was only about a mile away from where the Reed family lived from 1960 until 1995.)

From 1st July onwards, Eddie sent back misleading reports about where the bombs had fallen, and what damage they had inflicted. As my father wrote, "The Zigzag channel was considered indispensible to the bomb damage deception scheme."

But on 25th July this scheme of deception was brought to a halt. The first reason was that evening papers had started to print maps showing where the bombs had fallen: it is curious the censors did not stop them producing these maps. But in any case, we had got increasingly successful in blowing up the flying bombs while they were still in the air. Very few were now exploding on landing. But by this time, they had already killed over 6000 civilians, an appalling total for a wilfully indiscriminate weapon of mass destruction.

What was Eddie to do next? Ronnie took Eddie to lunch at the RAC Club. They discussed Eddie's idea to publish his memoirs, and Ronnie

The RAC Club at 89 Piccadilly, where Ronnie took Eddie to lunch. In 2011 it was celebrating the centenary of its move to these premises.

told him that was impossible. But the Germans had told Eddie about a new secret weapon they thought we had developed and fitted to some of our fighting ships. Called a "hedgehog", it was a mortar bomb which exploded in contact with a submarine, like a mine. For some time, the Germans had been puzzled that their U-boats were being caught and destroyed far more often than before. The real reason was that we were deciphering their naval codes. This was an even more complex code than the Enigma code. Because it was more complex, it was a year after decoding Enigma that we managed to decode the naval codes as well.

After that, Admiral Doenitz became so suspicious that we were so successful in tracking down and attacking his boats, he finally called a top level conference to discuss whether there was any way in which the British might be decoding naval messages. His experts said it was quite impossible: four rotors meant decipherment was virtually impossible: addition of the fifth rotor in the Enigma machine made it impossible. So he reluctantly decided it was a combination of bad luck, and possibly a traitor in the ranks.

Admiral Doenitz

On our side, the addition of the fifth rotor did make the messages even more difficult to decode. The solution emerged, when we started to get clues that the operators did not always use the fifth rotor. It was far easier for their operators to leave that one alone, and just use the other four, as they did normally. But of course, once we realised that was happening, we could treat the message as a normal one, coded with four rotors, and our decipherments continued almost as before.

The photo of the "hedgehog". What looks like a 6 inch ruler next to it, was actually 18 inches long. So we made the device look one third of its actual size, and impressed the Germans by our powers of "miniaturisation".

We knew that Doenitz must be puzzled at our success against his ships. We decided to increase the confusion by making the "hedgehog" appear to be a much more formidable weapon than it actually was. Apart from misleading them about its size, we got Eddie to tell them that each hedgehog was equipped with a proximity fuse, which exploded if it got anywhere near a submarine. This particularly applied to submarines diving in deep waters, he told them. In this way, we hoped to keep their submarines nearer the surface, which made it easier for us to pick them off.

But it was just at this point that Ronnie was posted as an intelligence liaison officer with the Americans in France. So he had to stop being Eddie's case officer, and another man was appointed to the post. On the day that Ronnie set off, Eddie presented him with a small parcel. It was his Iron Cross, a symbol both of their friendship and of the work they had done together. My father was very touched by this, and kept the Iron Cross safely. It is still in family hands.

The new Case Officer assigned to Eddie, Michael Ryde, was an officer of the old school. Puritanical and snobbish, he was also an alcoholic. At once, Ryde decided that this conman ex-criminal should be paid off and dismissed, and made it his task to ensure that that happened. One of his reports said that Chapman was "always in the company of beautiful women" – he may have thought that counted against him, but it sounds much more like jealousy.

In the National Archives there is a nice set of about ten photos, carefully labelled, showing the substantial damage caused by flying bombs to buildings in Central London. It was thought Eddie might take these photos (which are still apparently unpublished), back to Germany to impress them with his fact-finding. The note reproduced, which comments on this idea, was sent to Ryde from

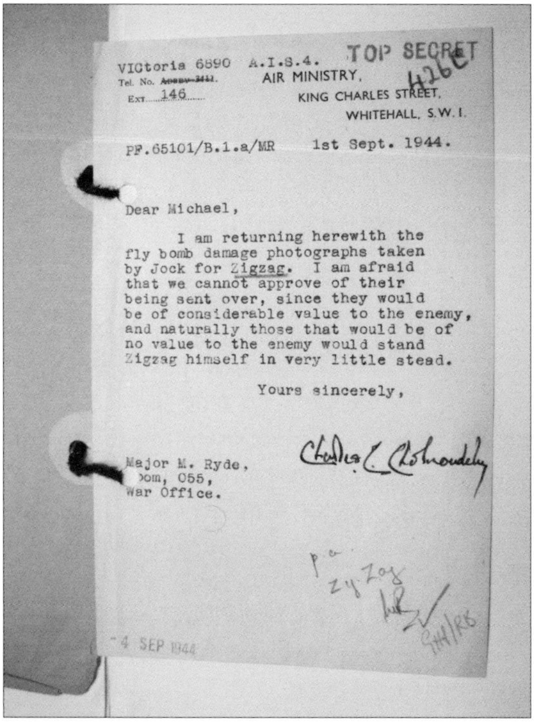

TOP SECRET

VICtoria 6890 A.I.S.4.
Tel. No. ~~Abbey 3411~~.
Ext. 146

AIR MINISTRY,
KING CHARLES STREET,
WHITEHALL, S.W. I.

PF.65101/B.1.a/MR 1st Sept. 1944.

Dear Michael,

I am returning herewith the fly bomb damage photographs taken by Jock for Zigzag. I am afraid that we cannot approve of their being sent over, since they would be of considerable value to the enemy, and naturally those that would be of no value to the enemy would stand Zigzag himself in very little stead.

Yours sincerely,

Charles C. Cholmondeley

Major M. Ryde,
Room, 055,
War Office.

4 SEP 1944

Charles Cholmondeley's note to Michael Ryde, saying that the photos taken would be of considerable value to the enemy, and so could not be sent to them.

Charles Cholmondeley, who you may remember was the prime originator of *Operation Mincemeat.* His chummy note is to "Michael": using his Christian name – very unusual among all these memos which use surnames the rest of the time. The photos, it seems, were taken by "Jock", presumably Jock Horsfall. No doubt, as MI5's top driver, Jock could drive anywhere and take photos, as long as he showed his identity card to any curious policeman. Cholmondeley scotches the idea of Eddie using the photos, because he says too much information would be revealed to the Germans.

But he adds the curious remark that "those (photos) that would be of no value to the enemy, would stand Zigzag himself in very little stead." This is untrue, and curious, because it undermines the whole concept of giving the Germans misleading information. As long as they believe it, one can continue the deception and build up their trust in their agent. If Eddie had been able to take even a few of these photos in central London, and bring them back to Germany, that would show the Germans how skilled, and trustworthy, he was. So why the curious remark? It seems quite likely that Michael Ryde had taken Cholmondeley out for a drink, put up the whole idea to him, and asked him to send him a note rubbishing the idea. This would add to Ryde's evidence for Chapman being both useless, and a liability.

Eventually Ryde managed to catch Chapman out. Late one evening

Ryde's deputy visited Chapman at home, and found him giving a lavish party. Various seedy friends from his past were there, including people like George Walker the boxer and boxing manager. When young, Walker had served two years for theft. He later became a millionaire businessman and Chairman of Brent Walker, which was behind the development of Brent Cross Shopping Mall. But his business enterprises later went bust. He was put on trial for theft and false accounting, but was eventually found not guilty.

Another friend from Eddie's past, who turned out not to be a friend, was Jimmy Hunt. He was his partner in crime and fellow safe-cracker in the 1930s, now finally released from a long spell in prison. When Ryde's deputy turned up at the party, Hunt got up from his chair and said to him, with a grin, "I suppose you have come to take Eddie away on a job." The implication was enough. Although conceivably the job might have just been a criminal job, set up by this unknown man, it seemed far more likely Eddie had told his friend about going on "secret missions for the government". This, along with other tiny slips, were enough for MI5 to accept Ryde's proposal that they should to terminate his employment with them. They did not even give him a golden handshake.

Since we have noticed this link-up between Zigzag and Mincemeat, with the same men being involved in both, it is intriguing to find a link with the United States as well.

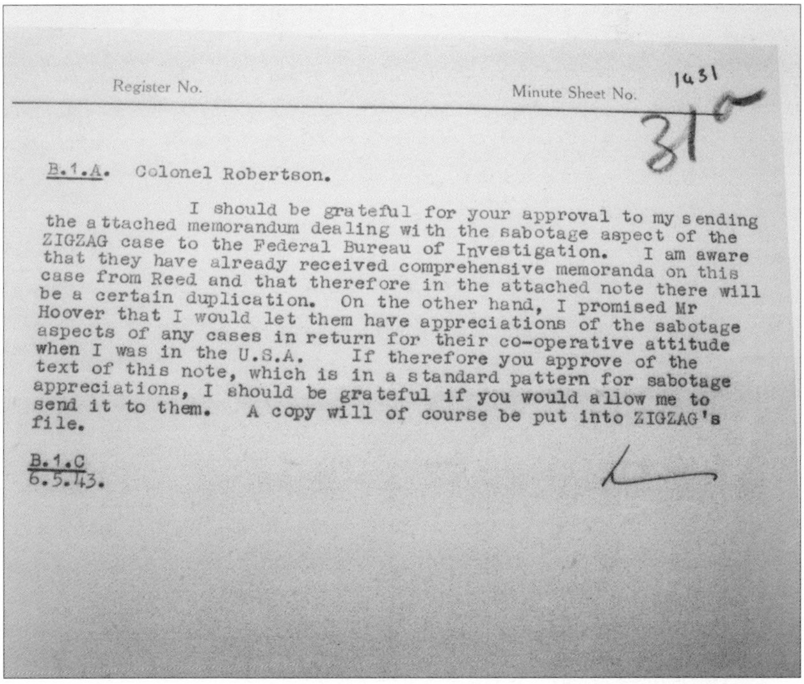
Register No. Minute Sheet No.

B.1.A. Colonel Robertson.

I should be grateful for your approval to my sending the attached memorandum dealing with the sabotage aspect of the ZIGZAG case to the Federal Bureau of Investigation. I am aware that they have already received comprehensive memoranda on this case from Reed and that therefore in the attached note there will be a certain duplication. On the other hand, I promised Mr Hoover that I would let them have appreciations of the sabotage aspects of any cases in return for their co-operative attitude when I was in the U.S.A. If therefore you approve of the text of this note, which is in a standard pattern for sabotage appreciations, I should be grateful if you would allow me to send it to them. A copy will of course be put into ZIGZAG's file.

B.1.C
6.5.43.

The memo from Guy Liddell, head of 'B' division of MI5, asking Tar Robertson if he can pass on details of Zigzag to the FBI.

Guy Liddell

It is a memo, dated June 1943, and apparently signed by Guy Liddell, to Tar Robertson, asking if he could pass on details of Zigzag's sabotage activities to the FBI. He adds that the FBI have already received "comprehensive memoranda on this case from Reed. On the other hand, I promised Mr Hoover that I would let them have appreciations of the sabotage aspects of any cases, in return for their co-operative attitude when I was in the USA." In 1931 Liddell moved from Scotland Yard to MI5, to become Deputy Director of Counter-Espionage. He visited the States both in 1936 and 1938, and in 1936 gave information to Edgar Hoover, Head of the FBI, which led to the break-up of a German spy ring operating both in the USA and across the Atlantic.

Shenley Lodge, Herts. Eddie's last and probably grandest house, which he and his wife ran as a health farm.

After the War, Eddie Chapman moved on to various business ventures, more or less sound, including a health farm. In 1966 he published his memoirs *The Real Eddie Chapman Story*, heavily censored. It was this which was the background for a film, *Triple Cross*, about his exploits as a double agent. It was produced by his old friend Terence Young in 1966, with Christopher Plummer as Eddie. Sadly, it is not a good film, with a feeble script. It is crying out for a remake. Eddie finally died at the end of 1997, aged 83.

TWELVE

OPERATION OVERLORD, GARBO AND D-DAY: 1944

MY FATHER mentioned above the deceptions carried out to try to get the Germans to believe that the Allied Invasion would be launched at Calais, rather than Normandy. And of course, the actual date was kept just as secret as the location. This knowledge was shared with very few, as its classification was even higher than Top Secret. For an obvious reason: if the Germans did get to find out the place and date of the Invasion, they would have all their forces ready and prepared to throw our forces back into the sea. It was vital for their forces to be kept back elsewhere. We have seen this happen earlier, where our deception Operation Mincemeat successfully kept the German forces unprepared, or waiting elsewhere, when we invaded Sicily in 1943. All the more essential to do this when we were invading France. The work done by Garbo and others was vital in having this effect after D-Day, with major tank divisions kept back in northeastern France when they should have been repelling our troops landing on the Normandy beaches.

The Bigots

The few people who were told in advance of the place and date of D-Day, were given a curious code-name. They were called Bigots (rather a topical term during the 2010 General Election, when Gordon Brown referred to a "bigoted woman"). On one occasion during the War, a ship's captain was showing King George VI round his ship, but carefully guided him away from a section which was curtained off. This was the section where the captain kept the plans and secrets of D-Day. When asked about this later, he said, "Well, how was I to know he was a Bigot?" And he meant it, of course, in the technical sense: he did not know that the King had been entrusted with the secrets of D-Day. It was my mother who told me that Ronnie was one of the Bigots. Obviously, he would need to be told about our plans for D-Day, as he was involved in the deception plans to mislead the Germans.

I continue with my father's memories.

"That [i.e. the use of double-agents] acted as the basic plan for the great deception plan, for Europe, to make the Germans think we were going to invade at Calais instead of at Normandy. This is set out in considerable detail in a book about a man called Garbo, who was the most remarkable double agent that ever operated during the war.

The double-agent Juan Pujol (Garbo) in one of his earlier disguises.

(*NR: Were you in charge of him?*) No, I wasn't. It was Cyril Mills of Bertram Mills Circus fame. But his principal man was a fellow called Tomas Harris, who was a Spaniard. Spoke perfect English – he owned a house right by the side of what was then our Headquarters, which was at Leconfield House in Curzon Street. We transmitted from his house and sent these messages across. Tommy unfortunately went back to Spain, was a mad keen racing driver and killed himself soon afterwards. All his recollections are set down in a book by Nigel West, together with all the recollections of Garbo, the double agent. Fascinating – well worth reading."

The double-agent Garbo got his name because he invented, and in effect acted the parts of, 24 spies which he declared were working for him in Britain. So in that respect, he was just as versatile as Greta Garbo!

Nigel West

[At this point, perhaps I could interrupt my father's narrative to say more about Nigel West. His book on Garbo the double agent was called simply *Garbo*, It was written by Juan Pujol, the real name of the agent, and Nigel West, and published by Weidenfeld and Nicholson in 1985. This continued Nigel West's series of books about the Security Service, in particular, his book *MI5*, published in 1981. My father told me he was very impressed by both the scholarship and the accuracy of his books. In the early 1990s, Nigel West tried several times to interview my father, or even just get him to comment on something he, Mr West, had written. But my father resolutely refused to do so, saying he was bound by the Official Secrets Act. On one occasion I visited him soon after another such refusal. He said that Nigel West had told him he was going to reproduce the Appendix my father had written for the official History of the Second World War. That had been published in 1990, but just said he was a "former MI5 officer". This time, Nigel West was going to name him, and did so, when he edited the *Faber Book of Espionage* (1993).

My mother also several times answered the phone to Mr West, and had to tell him that my father would not talk to him. Eventually Ronnie got so fed up with Nigel West ringing up, that he got in touch with his MP, Gerry Bowden, MP for Dulwich, and asked him to "get him off his back"!

Later, my father told me that he really did not want to be bothered by enquiries like that. He had spent almost all his working life dealing with security matters, and he wanted to enjoy his retirement dealing with other things. He also said he was worried that if he were to start revealing matters, thus breaking the Official Secrets Act, he might possibly lose his Civil Service pension. When I spoke to Nigel West about this, he said that was extremely unlikely. After all, even John Cairncross, who had admitted to spying for Russia, never had his pension taken away. I suspect another point my father had in mind was, that once he started commenting on his part in wartime activities, he would get more and more journalists wanting him to comment on or add to what they had written, and it would never stop. He just wanted a quiet life in retirement.

Having mentioned Nigel West's book on Garbo, one should say that the world really owes Mr West a great debt of gratitude over Garbo. Without his persistence, Garbo would have disappeared without trace. After the War, Juan Pujol was worried that some remaining Nazi might try to bump him off in revenge for what he had done. So he faked his own death in Angola in 1959, supposedly from malaria. Nigel West just had an instinct that might not be the end of the story.

It was when he was interviewing Anthony Blunt in 1981 that Blunt told him Garbo's name was Juan Garcia. Mr West suspected that was not the full name, and, when interviewing another SIS officer, he cleverly induced him to reveal the full name: Juan Pujol Garcia. He then got a researcher to go through all the Pujol Garcias in the Barcelona phone book. Eventually they found one who turned out to be Garbo's nephew, but he had last heard of his uncle in Venezuela. Nigel West then got another researcher based in Caracas to try all the Pujol Garcias there, and finally tracked down Garbo's son. And so, eventually, he managed to speak to Garbo, just in time to invite him back for the ceremonies marking the 40th anniversary of D-Day. Juan Pujol attended, was handed his MBE by the Duke of Edinburgh, and then had a reunion with wartime colleagues, including Tar Robertson and Cyril Mills, his first Case Officer.

It is immensely satisfying to find that justice was finally done to Garbo, our most important double-agent, and that he was briefly reunited with those who had worked with him during the War. All this underlines my own belief that it is the 40th, rather than the 50th anniversary, which is the most significant and useful anniversary to celebrate. On a 40th anniversary, enough time has gone by for people to appreciate the historical importance of what they are celebrating. Those who were in senior positions in their 30s and 40s, are now in their 70s and 80s, but happy to recall their part. Ten years later, many of those will have died, and those remaining are likely to have been too junior at the time to be able to contribute important memories. It is good that Garbo was tracked down in time for the 40th anniversary of D-Day.

THIRTEEN

SETTING OFF FOR FRANCE WITH THE AMERICANS

IN AUGUST 1944 my father was sent to France to liaise with an American intelligence unit, headed by Captain Tom Purner. Most of them were wireless specialists. Why was he sent to join the Americans? It seems likely they had already spotted Ronnie as someone who they could trust, and who had been in charge of several double-agents over the past three years. Through Guy Liddell, the Americans had been supplied with my father's reports on Zigzag. He was well qualified, then, to join an American group in administering occupied France and keeping an eye on possible sabotage from Nazis, as they reluctantly gave up the territory of the countries they had invaded.

Ronnie kept a series of sixteen photos of his, and the American, unit setting off from Chelsea Barracks. I reproduce some of them here. All the photos have detailed descriptions on the back, and all are dated 7th August 1944, so he went to France two months after D-Day.

An informal view of Ronnie in uniform, next to the lorry he was loading. Note he has a gun in the holster on his right leg. By this time, he had become Lieutenant Reed.

From left to right: Captain Patrick McElwee, CO of the British Unit, Lt. Ronnie Reed, and Côté – a French officer.

Captain Tom Purner, CO of the American Unit (centre) with Lieutenants Marshall and Reed. In this photo, Ronnie looks remarkably like Monty himself!

Ronnie Reed and Tom Purner supervise the loading of radio equipment at Chelsea Barracks.

Tom Purner supervises the loading of American vehicles outside 14 Ryder Street. Cockerille, Purner (centre) and Waith (presumably all Americans) outside 14 Ryder Street, loading up SCI 8 for France. Ryder Street must have been the American HQ.

Another view of vehicles loading up at 14 Ryder Street. Ironically, despite these photos being carefully labelled on the back, this one says, "SCI 9 and SCI 8 loading at Ryder Street."
Yet this vehicle is clearly SCI 10! On the vehicle behind can be read, "Caution. Left hand drive", which would be true, as it would be American, and on the left, "Speed Limit 40".

"Sergeant Oates on the motorcycle, with Corporal Harrewyn just behind him. They lead the column." Oates is driving either a Norton 16H, or a BSA M20. The lorry on the left is a Morris commercial personnel carrier.

All these photos show the Victorian buildings of Chelsea Barracks in 1944. They were demolished in the 1950s, and replaced by barracks built in tower blocks, so the photos are a useful record of their earlier state. The site has been unoccupied since 2008, when the troops were moved to Woolwich.

Detail of "my jeep" in another picture. Two men are visible, but neither of them are Ronnie. Confusingly, the man visible on the left is walking along, and is not on the vehicle.

The photo above is called "my jeep", so it should be Ronnie's. But the man sitting in the front of the vehicle is wearing a distinctive American cap, so perhaps it is Tom Purner, with Ronnie beside him. But Ronnie would hardly be driving a vehicle with left-hand drive. The simplest way to explain things is if this set of photos was taken by or for Tom Purner, so "my jeep" means Tom Purner's jeep. In that case, he is the man grinning at the camera, and his driver would be behind the windscreen. I explained above how the Americans may have suggested that Ronnie accompany them to France. But we do have a letter written by Ronnie to his boss in 1973, describing his wartime service.

"When the "second front" [i.e. the Invasion] was being planned, there was a requirement for a number of MI5/MI6 special Counter-

An informal portrait of Ronnie's friend Captain Tom Purner.

Intelligence units to round up agents and run double agents, using radio left behind by the enemy in Europe. MI5 and MI6 employees were needed to staff these units and, as I recall it, the one containing MI5 staff was called 104 S.C.I. Unit. I could only go into this army unit by taking a commission. So I went, with another civilian and two Intelligence Corps sergeants, Marshall and Plant (who were then employed by the Office in a civilian capacity) to a weekend W.O.S.B. [War Office Selection Board] somewhere in the north of England. [Photos kept by Ronnie show this was at Catterick Camp in Yorkshire.] I was accepted for a commission, gazetted as a lieutenant, and my pay was made up to my office pay. With the C.O. Major Harmer, three other officers and a number of O.R.s [other ranks] the unit was "mustered" with its transport and equipment at Chelsea Barracks. For administrative purposes the unit was attached to 21st Army group in BAOR and the unit went to France in July 1944. So far as I remember, in all other intelligence respects the unit reported back to the War Room in London, which was a joint MI5/6 Intelligence centre. We had our own ciphers, bags etc."

Ronnie gives these details, because he wrote this letter when there were reports of people's pensions being reduced because of a break in service. Someone, he thought, might argue that his two years in the Army 1944-6, would reduce his pension entitlement by two years.

As he put it, *"I took a commission in the Army in 1944 in order to continue the work of the Service, and at that time it never occurred to me that subsequently this might be construed as a "break" in my service to the Office. I was thirty years younger, immersed in the War, and the consideration of a pension was very far from my mind."* Presumably, for this 27-year-old, "surviving the War" was a rather higher priority!

FOURTEEN

THE LIBERATION OF PARIS

THE BATTLE FOR PARIS, followed by its Liberation, took place from 19th to 25th August 1944. My father reminisced about his time in France. This is the only part of his interview where he imitates a foreign accent, though he was very good at doing accents. In fact, my mother said that when they were courting, he would often put on a French accent, and she always went weak at the knees when he did!

"During the War, I was Liaison Officer with the Americans in a forest down somewhere south of Nantes, when Tom Purner, an American, heard that Paris had been liberated and said, "Rahnnie, we gotta go: we gotta go and see what's happened up in Paris." Fortunately he had a Jeep, and so we drove off at ten o'clock one night, all the way through up to Paris. I'd never been to Paris before.

The Trocadero, seen from the Eiffel Tower. Ronnie and Tom would have driven up the steps just visible between the two white buildings in the top centre.

"When we got to Paris we drove down l'Avenue de la Grande Armée, and there on the skyline was the Eiffel Tower and just in front of it was the Trocadero. We drove the jeep up the Trocadero steps, round and round, looking at the Eiffel Tower: the first time we'd ever seen Paris. It was a wonderful experience. Of course it was a hazardous time, because there were a lot of snipers about, and it was a bit dangerous, but there it is: they didn't get me!"

(*NR: You took over a room which had been occupied by a German, didn't you?*) "That was interesting, because we had to find ourselves accommodation. We used to look around for places the Germans had

De Gaulle walking up the Champs Elysees through liberated Paris. My father mentions there were still snipers about, and as de Gaulle was so tall, and could easily have been picked off, it was a brave action to walk through the streets like this before the snipers were eliminated.

occupied while they were in Paris. We eventually found a very luxurious flat. When we got into it, there was a notice on the dining room table saying, 'I have enjoyed my stay here enormously in Paris. I hope you will look after this place properly, because I shall be back.' Signed: Lt. Col. something or other. But I was with an American who spoke perfect German, and he decided to keep the card."

My father had a curious memory of one occasion when he stayed at Pontoise, NW of Paris, in 1945. It may have been while returning to London from "somewhere south of Nantes". I triggered off his memory in 1986 by saying I had recently been staying in Pontoise, while researching Pissarro, and had stayed in a local hotel which had "French toilets", i.e. the sort of hole in the concrete you used to expect in places like Turkey. But he was able to cap that. He said that in 1945 he too had stayed in Pontoise, at the Station Hotel. After his evening meal, he had asked the proprietor, "Où sont les toilettes?" "Where are the toilets?" The proprietor looked puzzled. "Oui, les toilettes?" said my father. The reply came back, "Mais Monsieur, il y a la cour." "But Sir, there's a courtyard outside." And that was what everyone had to use!

In February 1945 Ronnie was in Brussels. He kept the theatre program, published in English, "for the Military Man's entertainment". It was of the Theatre Royal de la Monnaie, where he saw a performance of Samson and Delilah, by Saint Saens, on 25th February 1945. The theatre's name means "The Royal Theatre of the Mint". It was built on Napoleon's orders, and opened by him in 1800.

Ronnie's postcard of the Paris Opera House.

Ronnie seems to have spent about a year in France and Belgium, from August 1944 until the spring of 1945. We have a postcard he sent to Mary Dyer (later his wife) on 18th April 1945. It shows the Paris Opera House on the front, and refers to the opera "Le Roi d'Ys" by Lalo. On the back the card reads,

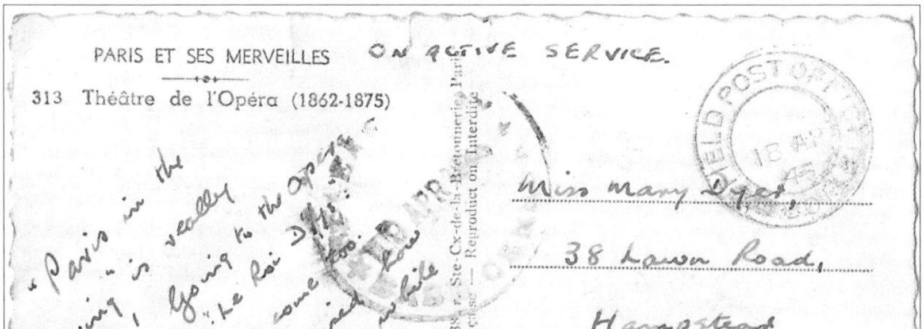

PARIS ET SES MERVEILLES

313 Théâtre de l'Opéra (1862-1875)

ON ACTIVE SERVICE.

"Paris in the Spring" is really delightful! Going to the opera tonight to see "Le Roi D'Ys". Do wish you could come too. You would be surprised how often I think about you while I am here.

Much love,

Ronnie

Editions d'Art GUY, 38 r. Ste-Cx-de-la-Bretonnerie, Paris
Fabrication Française — Reproduction Interdite

FIELD POST OFFICE 18 AP 45

Miss Mary Dyer,
38 Lawn Road,
Hampstead,
London, N.W.3

The back of Ronnie's postcard.

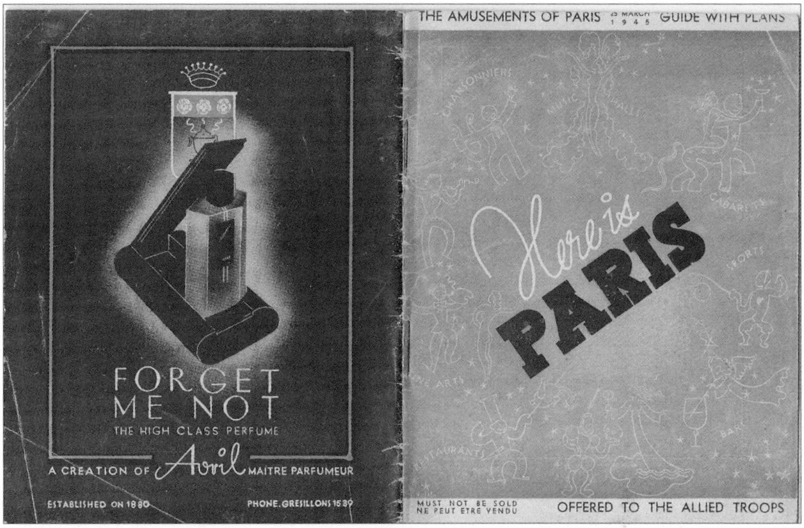

A guide to the amusements of Paris, produced for the Allied Troops in 1945.

"'Paris in the spring' is really delightful! Going to the opera tonight to see "Le Roi d'Ys". Do wish you could come too. You would be surprised how often I think about you while I am here.

Much love, Ronnie"

He carefully kept a booklet entitled "Here is Paris: A guide to the Amusements of Paris". This booklet was published every two weeks, apparently by the Canadian Army Education Services, and issued for British and Canadian Forces. It was "Offered to the Allied Troops" but "Must Not Be Sold." This copy is dated March 1945, and lists all the theatres and what they were showing, the movies on view, and the cabarets.

You might have thought that he would have found out about the opera from it. However, under Theatres it says, "For the Comedie-Francaise, the Opera and the Opera Comique, please consult advertisements."

No doubt he did.

A careful reading of Ronnie's postcard suggests he was based in Paris for a time, and not just visiting. "You would be surprised how often I think about you while I am here" does not suggest a day trip. But his 1973 letter to his boss says:

"I worked in Belgium and then Germany with the [S.C.I.] unit which subsequently became part of No 7 Civil Control Unit (an MI6 unit) which then came under the control of the Intelligence Division in Bad Salzuflen in Germany, under Sir Dick (then Brigadier) White. He invited me to continue to work for the Office when I returned to England after the war."

FIFTEEN

RONNIE IN GERMANY AND AUSTRIA, SECOND HALF OF 1945

IT APPEARS THAT Ronnie spent the first half of 1945 in French-speaking areas such as Brussels, Paris and the "forest somewhere south of Nantes". The last we see of him there is the photo below, taken in Brussels in April 1945. But soon after that he followed the Americans into Germany.

(NR: Later on you were in Frankfurt for a time, weren't you?)

"Frankfurt am Main – yes. We went down, again, with the Americans down there, with Tom Purner, and we decided the best place to have as a headquarters was the champagne factory, because only half of it had been bombed. One half we could operate as a champagne factory and the other half we could use as offices." *(NR: So you could drink the champagne while going about your work.)* "Yes."

To put this into context. Wiesbaden (where we next find Ronnie) was captured by US Army forces on 28th March 1945. They launched their attack across the Rhine from Mainz at 1am. By the end of the

It was in Brussels that this photograph was taken, in April 1945. It shows him in uniform, and was the official photo taken for the Office.

day the two forces of the 80th US Infantry Division had captured 900 German soldiers, for the loss of only three dead and three missing. They had also captured a warehouse full of 4000 cases of champagne. There are two such factories in Wiesbaden now: one is in the centre, the other, the Jacquart factory, is on the main road out of Wiesbaden to Frankfurt. That would explain why Ronnie refers to it being in Frankfurt when the photos that show him were taken in Wiesbaden. In fact, the US Seventh Army had its HQ in Frankfurt, so he may have moved from one base to the other.

US forces have never left Wiesbaden: the US 1st Armored Division has its headquarters at Wiesbaden Army Airfield, just off the road for Frankfurt. And indeed even more Americans are moving to Wiesbaden now that their other bases like Darmstadt and Heidelberg are closing down. In fact the 1st Armored Division is scheduled to move back to Texas in 2011, to make way for US Army Europe.

Three photos, one letter and one article survive of Ronnie's time in Germany and Austria, in the second half of 1945. The first photo was taken in Wiesbaden.

This photo shows Ronnie with a watering-can, filling up the radiator of his car. The photographer captioned this "Ronnie watering his Mrs Miniver". Ronnie dated it to August 1945, Wiesbaden. Mary added the comment, "Note the pool of water under the radiator!"

Ronnie called his car "Mrs Miniver". The Film *Mrs Miniver*, starring Greer Garson, was released in 1942. In the USA, its gross takings were the highest of any MGM film up to that time. Likewise, in Britain, it was named the top box office attraction of 1942. In the film, Mrs Miniver is outstandingly capable, and rises to any challenge. Hence, presumably, her name is used for the car.

This photo is captioned "Major R T Reed!" It presumably shows the car assigned to him once he became a Major. This car has a different army number from the earlier one, and also has a roof rack.

Ronnie Reed standing in front of his new car, with Diana Hankey. She may have been related to the first Lord Hankey. Maurice Hankey (b. 1877) served as the very first Cabinet Secretary from 1916 to 1938. After being ennobled in 1939, he served in the War Cabinet under both Chamberlain and Churchill. In 1940 he wrote a report which gave the SIS (MI6) a clean bill of health. The first car Ronnie actually bought in civilian life, was in 1952. It was a Ford 8, and had the number-plate BTP 666. The car above seems to be a Humber Super-Snipe.

We also have a letter written by Ronnie in September 1945. It reads as follows:

322182 Captain RT. Reed
British Liaison Officer
OSS Mission for Germany
A.P.O. 655, US Army

Saturday 15th September (1945)

"Gay Vienna"

My Dear Mary,

How hollow sounding is the phrase "Gay Vienna" today. The same story as in all the European towns appears once more – a tale of destruction, desolation and disease. The poverty, pimps and prostitutes. Rubble-filled streets with miserable rabbits of human beings scurrying amongst it, piling up a few bricks here, boarding up a window there, and around it all an atmosphere of hopelessness and resignation to intolerable conditions.

This is my second day in Vienna. I am leaving tomorrow morning for the Austrian Tyrol and then back to the Rhine. I wanted to write to you because you were very much with me last night, and today.

A party of us went to a sort of night club yesterday evening. It was really no more than a glorified café (except for the prices). We listened to a second rate cabaret and had a table next to two Russian officers who were with two women; one about 25 and the other 40 years old. I thought I recognised the type of older woman. "Procuress" is the name. The younger one looked so much like you. Dark and – well you know your own self.

Vienna's Opera House, as it is now.

"One of my party translated the conversation between the Russians and the older woman. They were working out the price of the girl in marks and cigarettes while she was attempting to push up the price by acting provocatively. When she stood up to watch the cabaret I saw that she was about 4 months gone with child. Life is horrid on occasions.

You see when I first looked at her and did not know what they were saying I thought of you and missed you. And then I heard what they were saying and she stood up...

And I thought of the times I had made love to you and how lovely it was together, and how our relationship had been so healthy and clean and delightful. When we listened to some Mozart together and kissed softly and went to sleep...

I could not believe that at that moment it was simply a question of marks and cigarettes – and she stood up. Like tearing the Mona Lisa or pouring nitric acid over your face and lips that I have kissed so many times and want to now.

"The Opera Hall in Vienna has been destroyed. The Opera is playing somewhere else. We tried to get in (I am told it is very good), but failed (just like Sadlers Wells, all booked up until Monday!), but we did succeed in getting to the Ballet which is being held in a small, or fairly small, concert hall something of the size of the Wigmore Hall, only much more elaborate. Would be first class for chamber music recitals. The Ballet I had never seen before. There were four obscure Italian pieces which I could describe but not pronounce. Orchestra first-rate, dancing very elementary, beautiful costumes, fascinating girls and intelligent acting. I am going to try and come back here soon again to see the Opera.

It's getting late now (0700 am). I do so miss you.

Ever yours,

Ronnie

PS: 1. Have you turned into a cat again?

2. Did you kiss Conchita for me?

3. Sorry about grammar and writing. But you ought to think yourself damned lucky I write at all – darling!

That is the only detailed letter which survives from Ronnie in Germany. Perhaps one should explain that Conchita was Mary's cat. She was possibly named after the world-famous soprano Conchita Supervia. Supervia died in childbirth at the tragically early age of 41. This was in 1936, which may have been the year that Mary acquired her cat.

As for the Vienna Opera House, it was greatly damaged by bombing in March 1945, and finally reopened in 1955. Until then, the State Opera was temporarily housed at the Theater an der Wien, which may have been the "fairly small concert hall" which Ronnie refers to.

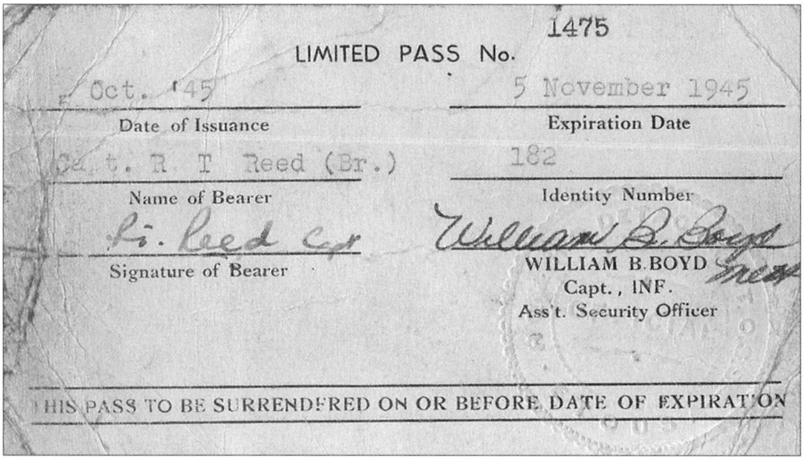

LIMITED PASS No. 1475

Oct. '45
Date of Issuance

5 November 1945
Expiration Date

Capt. R T Reed (Br.)
Name of Bearer

182
Identity Number

Signature of Bearer

WILLIAM B. BOYD
Capt., INF.
Ass't. Security Officer

THIS PASS TO BE SURRENDERED ON OR BEFORE DATE OF EXPIRATION

Ronnie's Security Pass for October 1945, presumably used when he was serving in Germany. Note it states he is "Br." i.e. British, and gives his rank as Captain.

Lastly, an article written on Christmas Day 1945, which Ronnie presumably thought of submitting for publication.

25th December 1945

London: Impressions on Leave from the Rhine Army

What is it about London that makes it so enchanting? On a logical basis no-one could possibly want to stay here now. Queues, difficulties of travelling, food and drink shortage, lack of paint; one can hardly imagine WANTING to stay compared with Rhine Army Headquarters. There we have all we require. We can drink to our heart's content, eat every night on a pre-war standard, be clothed, warmed and waited on, yet we reject it in favour of this.

"People do not look well here. They appear to these Army eyes to look cold, miserable and disappointed. The first few months of peace have not brought the millennium. Do they think it was a hollow victory? I wonder if it would help to organise visits to Germany? Would the sight of the vanquished's sufferings throw the victor's blessings into relief? I recently wrote on the subject of Reparations:-

"Pregnant women, queues, string bags
Rubble dust and rain, old rags
My Germany of music, culture
Am I now to be a vulture?"

"That's probably why one wants to come back to London. This is a living city. The dead bones of the scarred and shattered dwellings are not rattling every day. Here the constant crowds are breathing new life into them, the new windows do not glare hostility; they wink as you pass by. The twisted girders are not poised to strike; they wave at you. Posters do not warn, they invite.

"Old friends, old faces, old places – they are still here. This is the corner where I met you last summer. This is the street where we dodged the flying bomb. Flying bomb. That seems an awful long time ago. It fell just here. But there is an exhibition in the gap it left. In Germany the place is filled with weeds and black water. London. In the spring when the crocuses are peeping through and the parks are singing, I'm coming back to you."

That spring he did indeed come back to London, because that is when he married Mary Dyer.

SIXTEEN

A YOUNG MARRIED MAN, AFTER THE WAR

MY FATHER'S INTERVIEW continues: "After that I was questioned on going back to the BBC and becoming involved in television. But The Office said to me, "If you would like to stay, we would like to keep you." So I stayed with them, didn't go back to the BBC and they put me in charge of the dissolution of what was called the War Room. I think this was really a test, because until that time I'd only been involved in the technical side, with radio stuff. They wanted to see how I made out on the administrative front, which, presumably, I was all right at. Because thereafter, in my time in the security service, I used to oscillate between having charge of the small scientific laboratories and directing their work, because I knew about radio, or dealing with other aspects of the work of the security service."

Ronnie and Mary got married on 15th June 1946. Shortly afterwards, they stayed in Paris on holiday. But my mother was very firm that it was not a honeymoon: the Reeds were not going to be so conventional as to have one of those!

A photo of Mary, taken in the Bois de Boulogne in May 1946, during their holiday there. My mother told me that this was the photo my father kept in his wallet to look at, when he was abroad.

Just over a year later their elder son Nicholas (myself) was born on 15th July 1947. Their second son Adrian, named after Sir Adrian Boult, was born on 17th October 1949. They had planned to have more children, and Mary said it would have been nice to have a daughter in addition to us two. However, she had always suffered from asthma, and this was in the days before steroids. After having her first child, her asthma got worse; after having Adrian it got severely worse, and the doctors told her that a third child might well cause her death from asthma. (The threat was real: not long after, the film star Robert Donat died from asthma.) So they stuck to two.

They had not planned to have children quite so soon, and finance was tight for some years. Actually, my mother told me that she had been practising the Marie Stopes method of birth control, and it failed, with me. When she fell pregnant, they thought seriously about having an abortion, as their finances were so tight. It would have to be illegal, but could be carried out, for a price, on the grounds of the mental health of the woman. As one spokesman for the BMA put it, "Before the 1967 Abortion Act, we already had abortion on demand – but the demand was £300." Then my parents sat down and considered matters.

Ronnie and Nicholas in about 1950.

They finally decided that the process had started, a new potential life had begun and that, if necessary, they would forego any luxuries while having children. For over ten years our only holidays were taken in the car, using two tents to stay in fields or camping sites overnight.

I know of one campaigner against abortion, who was motivated mainly by the knowledge that his poor, one-parent mother, might have chosen to have an abortion, had it been legal, and then he would never have been born. This prospect so horrified him that he wanted to prevent anyone taking the "wrong" decision. On the other hand, I wish (not very hard) that my mother had had me aborted, and started with my brother two years later. Then I, born four years later, would have had the advantages of better health care, no rationing, quite possibly no asthma, and perhaps three inches taller as well! I might even have been female. Or, on the other hand, not. The moral of all this is that you cannot take moral decisions purely on hypothetical alternatives. After all, the past cannot be changed – except under a totalitarian regime.

Ronnie's mother was a War Widow, giving her enough to live on, but no money for luxuries, or to help her son. Mary's father was himself widowed, and then remarried twice. So the Reeds inherited nothing to help them set up house: almost all our furniture was bought from second-hand shops. Some of it, such as the dining-room table and a chest of drawers, came from Heals, and other furniture from Austins in Peckham. We lived in rented flats until 1957, first in 14(b) Belsize Lane, Hampstead NW3, and then, from 1952, at 12 Mowbray Road, Upper Norwood SE19, where we finally had a back garden where my brother and I could play. It was in 1954 that Ronnie bought our first car, a Ford 8, and used it regularly to visit his mother in Hampstead, and to visit Mary's father and third wife in North Holmwood, near Dorking, Surrey.

SEVENTEEN

THE MEN (AND WOMEN) WHO SPIED FOR RUSSIA

MY FATHER continued, "In 1951 I was put in charge of the counter espionage service against the Russians, which was really fascinating, because I was therefore in charge of cases like Klaus Fuchs, Donald MacLean, Guy Burgess, Kim Philby – all the other famous and infamous spies, but not George Blake, I'm glad to say. (*NR: Presumably you didn't interrogate them but you were in charge.*) I was in charge of arranging all the investigation of what they said."

Klaus Fuchs: the nuclear spy

Background: Klaus Fuchs was born in Germany in 1911. While he was at Kiel University, he joined the student communist party in 1932, and was beaten up by Nazi Brownshirts. The following year, Hitler's Nazis burned down the Parliament building, the Reichstag, then blamed the communists and launched a purge against them, as well as the Jews. Fuchs soon left the country and made his way to England, where he continued his studies at Bristol University, and then in Edinburgh. While he was in Bristol, the German consul told the police that Fuchs was a Communist, but the authorities decided this was simply a Nazi slur. Though briefly interned as an enemy alien at the start of the War, he was such a brilliant student that his professor arranged for him to get a job in Birmingham which required secrecy. Fuchs duly signed the Official Secrets Act in May 1941 and went to work for the innocent-sounding Tube Alloys Project. This was actually the British nuclear programme. Later that year, he walked up to the entrance of the Russian Embassy and volunteered to pass on to them any information they might find useful. They accepted his offer.

Klaus Fuchs

Within the year, the unanimous support of his supervisors led to him getting British citizenship. Once again, the "Nazi slur", that he was a communist, was ignored, despite being true.

He then continued to pass on atomic secrets to the Russians, both when he worked in England as well as the States. He watched the first atomic bomb test, and passed on to the Russians, all the information he had about the two bombs dropped on Hiroshima and Nagasaki. Soon after that, he was accepted as the top British nuclear scientist at the British atomic research establishment at Harwell. But within a couple of years, the British realised a spy had been at work, and deduced he was the man. That was when Jim Skardon was sent to Harwell to try to extract a confession. My father told me he was the person to whom Jim Skardon reported on his various interviews with Fuchs. Here my father's interview continues:

Jim Skardon as I remember him, with his pipe and moustache.

"One investigator [I worked with] was Jim Skardon, an ex-Scotland Yard man, who gave me a lot of help, and is now dead. The most amazing case was Klaus Fuchs, the atomic spy (who worked with Nunn May), because Fuchs said that he had never done anything for the Russians at all. He was interrogated by Jim Skardon down at Harwell. There he said that he was very fond of England. He was glad the Russians had won the war, as we were, because we had cooperated with them, but that he had never had done anything of which he had been ashamed, and eventually Jim went off to lunch with him. Fuchs had been rather quiet at lunch, and when he came back he said, "I think it would be best if I told you about it." (*NR: How did he persuade him?*) He didn't persuade him. He just decided that if he lost his job at Harwell, the British remaining atomic energy effort had ended, so he could better help Britain by cooperating. (*"So he was almost turned, in a way."*) In a way, in a way. So it was a fascinating time, and lots of interesting cases.

I should add that my father carefully cut out and kept Skardon's obituary from The Times of 1987. For those who want to know more about the thought processes which led Fuchs to change his mind and confess, one cannot do better than read "The Traitors" by Alan Moorehead, published in 1952.

The Cambridge Spy Ring: Philby, Burgess and MacLean

Just to remind the reader. It emerged in the 1960s that a group of Cambridge graduates had infiltrated MI5 and MI6 and successfully spied for Russia from the early 1940s. All five had been students at Cambridge University in the 1930s, where they joined an undergraduate group called The Apostles, led by the charismatic don Anthony Blunt.

Said my father, "I think pretty well everything has come out in all the books (and there are *many* of them) that have been written about the Cambridge Spy Ring."

Burgess and Maclean

Guy Burgess and Donald Maclean were the first two spies in this group, to be suspected of spying for Russia. Guy Burgess was a flamboyant homosexual, Donald Maclean probably bisexual, though he married and had children. Guy Burgess went into the Foreign Office and was later posted to Washington. While there, he handed over many important documents to someone at the Russian Embassy. Donald Maclean, son of a famous Labour Cabinet Minister, Sir Donald Maclean, also joined the Foreign Office after Cambridge.

Beaconshaw, home of the Macleans in the 1950s (left), Beaconshaw in 2011 (right)

His home was an attractive Victorian house called Beaconshaw. It is just outside Tatsfield, Surrey, where he lived with his wife Melinda and their two children. However, MI5 already had suspicions about Maclean's loyalty. They had him tailed when he walked around London, to see if he met a Russian "friend", or even left messages at pre-arranged spots. My father told me that he also assigned someone to follow Maclean back from work to his home in Tatsfield. He said it was quite difficult to do that, as there were not many London workers commuting from Tatsfield, but the job was done successfully.

Before he married in 1940, Maclean was intimately involved with a woman called Kitty Harris. She was born in London, but grew up in Canada and Chicago. In Chicago she became a communist, and married a Communist Party organiser called Earl Browder. After a couple of years, she left her husband, moved to Europe and became a KGB Agent. In 1937 she was in London when she was assigned to "look after" Donald Maclean. He used to remove top secret papers from the Foreign Office and take them to her flat late at night. She would photograph them there, and he would return them the following morning. Maclean was six foot tall, blond, and the ultimate British aristocrat. It did not take long for their affair to start. And, of course, she duly reported their affair to her controllers in Moscow. She explained, in fact, that they began and ended every meeting with sex. Sometimes this seems to have affected their work. A telegram from Moscow complained, "The material in the last two pouches turned out to contain only half of each image. What was the problem? Moreover, in the last batch, many of the pages were almost out of focus." Can we perhaps guess why?

In 1938 Maclean was moved to Paris. He asked if Kitty could stay as his contact, and the KGB agreed to send her out there as well. The relationship lasted until 1940, when the Germans invaded Paris. Kitty was then sent out to Mexico and, after the War, retired to Moscow. By that time Maclean had met another lady, called Melinda.

Donald Maclean met Melinda Marling in January 1940, in a café on the Left Bank called the Café de Flore, or Flora's Cafe. Its great rival was Les Deux Magots: The Two Moneybags. In both cafés, intellectuals and radicals flourished. In the Café de Flore, Communists met fellow-communists, and there was an Anglophile community as well. Donald and Melinda fitted both categories. Daughter of the wealthy Mrs Melinda Dunbar, of Boston and New York, Melinda began an affair with Donald, but she became bored with this upper-crust aristocratic conservative. Eventually, to win her back, he confided that he was actually a communist and a spy. His confession worked; they were married in June 1940, and came straight to England, just

The Café de Flore, in Paris, where Donald met Melinda. It still retains much of its art deco interior unchanged from the 1940s. It gets its name from a small statue of the goddess Flora which stood opposite it. Melinda was staying in the hotel next door.

before the Germans occupied Paris. They stayed in London until the end of the War, then in 1948 Donald became head of the chancery at the British embassy in Cairo. His Russian contact, Modin, used to meet him in the Arab quarter of Cairo. Tall blonde Maclean waiting for his contact among the Arabs was about as conspicuous as you could get. It's only surprising he was never reported. But then Maclean suggested that his wife should pass on the stolen documents to Modin's wife at the hairdressers. Melinda was very happy to do this, and it worked well. We now know that, over the course of his spying career, Maclean handed over the contents of 45 boxes of documents to the Russians.

On Friday 25th May 1951, Maclean and Burgess suddenly left Britain, and the suspicion was that they had fled to Moscow. In fact, there had been a top secret meeting on the Friday, when it was decided to bring Maclean in for interview on Monday the 28th. But they fled that Friday evening. Burgess had spotted that they could take a day trip by ferry from Southampton to St Malo, without needing passports. They would simply fail to rejoin the ship coming back from France. But why did they leave so hurriedly on the Friday? Someone must have tipped them off. Who was that someone: the Third Man in this tale? We shall return to that in a moment.

The first thing MI5 knew about the disappearance of the two diplomats was on the Monday morning, when Melinda Maclean rang the Foreign Office, asking if anyone had seen her husband. She explained that he had left hurriedly on Friday night with another man, and had not been home since. Soon after, an Austin A40 car left on the dock at Southampton was identified as having been hired by Guy Burgess. MI5 realised immediately how significant this was, and Sir Dick White, Head of MI5, agreed to fly straight to France to try to intercept them. Having got to Heathrow, he then found his passport was out of date, and had to wait some time for it to be renewed. By then, the fugitives were well away.

In the middle of August 1951, my father was sent down to Tatsfield to interview Mrs Maclean, who repeated that she knew nothing about

Left: Melinda and her daughter "Pinkers" in the garden, after Donald's disappearance. Note the pepper-grinder – something much more common in the USA than in Britain in 1951. *Right:* A modern view of the sitting room in which my father interviewed Mrs Maclean after her husband's disappearance.

Donald's disappearance. My mother remembered that some of the tabloids complained about this "brutal" treatment by a security officer (my father) interrogating this poor innocent woman, who had no idea what had, or might have, happened to her husband. According to a contemporary report, my father "grilled Melinda on the most intimate details of her life with Donald. He suggested that she knew all along that Donald was a Communist, was probably a Communist herself, and was going off to join him." Melinda flared up in what appeared to be anger. "You have proved nothing against my husband. Until you do, I shall never believe he was a traitor to this country."

Melinda kept up a very good pretence of ignorance. But, as we have seen, in fact she knew all about her husband's activities, and had assisted him with them in Cairo. Two years after his disappearance, she and the family joined him in Moscow.

Left: The Macleans with their two boys at the back of Beaconshaw. *Right:* the back of the house in 2011, with the sitting-room on the left. Its window was enlarged after 1953.

Kim and Litzi Philby

Kim Philby was probably the most important of those who spied for Russia. He was so well regarded in Britain he rose to become Deputy Head of MI6, the department which dealt with our spies abroad.

Kim Philby in 1956, just after the Prime Minister had "cleared" him of spying.

Philby's introduction to communism was really through his first girlfriend, who became his wife. Litzi Friedman was an active communist in Vienna. Philby had just finished his degree at Cambridge, and was keen to witness how the communists were fighting fascism in Vienna. In 1933 he went to stay in the Friedman household, and there met their daughter, Litzi. She introduced him to everything: including sex. We are told they first made love in the snow on a side street in freezing Vienna, heated by the touch of flesh on flesh. Philby said to a later girlfriend, "I know it sounds impossible, but it was actually quite warm once you got used to it." The following year, there were street fights between communists and fascists in Vienna, and Litzi was in danger. Finally Philby rescued her the most effective way: by marrying her then taking her back to London. There she contacted a KGB operative, who recruited Philby. And Philby then recruited his friends for the Russians as well. So you could say the real recruiter for the Russians was Philby's wife Litzi. When Philby started to assume his new persona as a right-wing fascist supporter, he felt obliged to separate from her. He could then say to the British that his communism had been a "youthful aberration."

My father summed up his view of Philby. "Philby I knew well. Nobody, ever, anywhere, thought he was likely to be a spy, and he nearly went to the top of MI6 as head of MI6, because he was so good. He gave no indication whatsoever that he was operating for the Russians. That was *fantastic*. Even people like Sir Dick White and Lord Rothschild, and all those who knew him equally well, found it *very* difficult to believe. Lord Rothschild said he found it almost impossible to believe that Philby had been a Russian spy, which of course he was, for years and years."

(*NR: "And he wrote all about it when he was in Russia."*).

A poster for The Third Man. It culminates in a chase through the sewers of Vienna. Modern tourists can, if they wish, visit the sewers where it was filmed.

"He wrote all about it: his book is quite untrue. Pure propaganda. *My Silent War*, it was called". (*NR: "When you say it's propaganda, though, if he's talking about how he successfully infiltrated, presumably that's generally true."*) "Well, he didn't write about that. He never gave the impression that he was responsible for the deaths of very large numbers of people, because he gave their identities to the Russians, and it's amazing."

Although we knew about Philby's treachery in 1956, we still did not have enough evidence to convict him. So instead, my father said, the Office no longer provided him with any secret material, and he came to realise he could do no more for Russia. Eventually, in 1963, he fled to Russia.

We mentioned earlier the mystery of the Third Man, who must have tipped off Burgess and Maclean in 1951. The title *The Third Man* became well known once the film, now widely regarded as a classic, came out in 1949. The film was directed by Carol Reed, and starred Joseph Cotton and Orson Welles. Much of it was filmed in the ruins of bomb-damaged Vienna. It was based on a novella by Graham Greene, but immediately turned by Greene into a screenplay. In the film, the missing Harry Lime is supposed to have been killed in a road accident, witnessed by two others. But his friend (played by Joseph Cotton) starts to hear rumours that there was a third man on the scene, and he goes to look for this mysterious Third Man. He eventually turns out to be the missing Harry Lime (played by Orson Welles). We now know that it was Kim Philby who tipped off Burgess that Maclean was about to be arrested. So it was Philby who was The Third Man whom everyone was looking for.

But here we come to the most remarkable coincidence of all in this "strange and eventful tale". Graham Greene, who wrote the story, had himself been in MI6. (He used his experiences as background for his novel *Our Man in Havana*) While Greene was in MI6, his boss was a certain Kim Philby. And when Greene came to describe the character of The Third Man in the film, he based it on Philby. So Philby was The Third Man both in fiction, and in fact!

On one occasion, probably in the 1970s, when I had been reading about Philby, I asked my father why it was that Macmillan had completely exonerated him from any suspicion of wrong-doing, when in fact the Security Service were virtually certain that Philby had been a spy. My father said that Macmillan's statement had surprised him. The PM could have said there was no evidence to indicate that Philby was a spy, rather than, in effect, implying that Philby was completely innocent of all accusations. The difficulty lay in "clearing" him, without stating that he had never been a spy. My father clearly thought that Macmillan had gone too far the other way.

The Fourth Man: Anthony Blunt

When we come to the Fourth Man, the author Andrew Boyle found out the truth before he wrote *The Climate of Treason*, published in 1979. His was the story of the three spies Philby, Burgess and Maclean, and he would have liked to have named the two other spies, i.e. the Fourth and Fifth Men. In 1964 Anthony Blunt, by now Sir Anthony Blunt, Surveyor of the Queen's Pictures, confessed to MI5 that he had been a spy, handing secrets to the Russians during the War. But he only agreed to talk to them, on condition that the Security Service agreed to give him immunity from prosecution. Boyle knew this, but when he approached Blunt, Blunt threatened to sue Boyle for libel if he even suggested that he had been a spy. He presumably counted on the fact that the Establishment would stick by their word and always cover up for him. So Boyle felt compelled to keep quiet about Blunt, and had to use the pseudonym "Maurice" when referring to Blunt in his book.

I remember in 1979 when The Times alleged that the Fourth Man was a Cambridge lecturer called Donald Beves. When I asked my father about this, he said it was quite ridiculous to suggest him. There

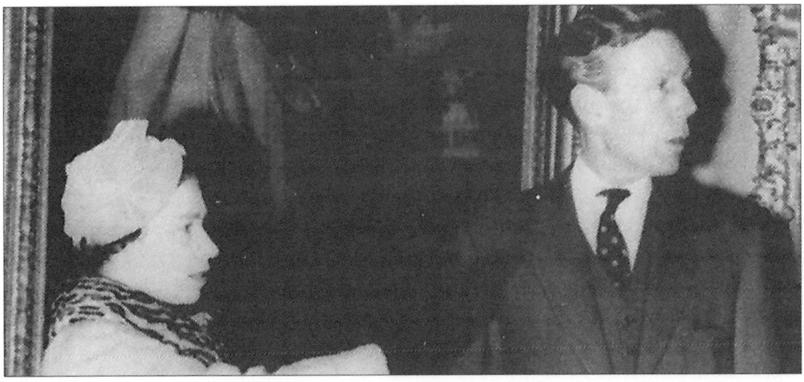

Sir Anthony Blunt, when he was Surveyor of the Queen's Pictures

was no evidence at all that it might have been Beves. (Of course, my father knew who it actually was, but did not say he did.) Looking back, one assumes that someone knew the truth and wanted to tip off The Times. So he presumably said that the man was someone who had been a Cambridge lecturer in the thirties, who was also homosexual, and whose name had five letters beginning with B. Remarkably, two men fitted that description. One was Beves. Perhaps someone thought it could not possibly be Blunt, and that left only Beves as the other possibility. But it is quite possible that the clues were left, to see if it flushed out the real name.

Andrew Boyle's book. On the front cover, it showed Maclean (above), with Philby bottom right, and Burgess next to him.

Boyle's book, revealing "Maurice" as a traitor, was published on 4th November 1979. His book led to an immediate debate as to why two of the traitors should have got away scot-free. Four days later, good old Private Eye decided to take the substantial risk of identifying "Maurice" as Blunt. Even before her election Mrs Thatcher had been informed that the Fourth Man had in fact been discovered, and that it was Sir Anthony Blunt, who was now Surveyor of the Queen's Pictures. She was furious that Blunt had not only got away with it, had received no punishment, but had even kept his knighthood for "services to his country". On 15th November 1979, Mrs Thatcher revealed to the Commons that Blunt was in fact a confessed spy. It is to Mrs Thatcher's credit that she decided that this cover-up and complete immunity from prosecution was a step too far. The following day, the Daily Mail and The Guardian, two papers rarely in agreement, were united in saying that what had happened earlier had "the stench of hypocrisy and Establishment cover-up." Shortly afterwards, Blunt lost his job as Surveyor of the Queen's Pictures, and had his knighthood revoked.

Blunt relied on the fact that his colleagues would never reveal his role. His justification for his behaviour gives in interesting insight into his motivation. He said, "If I were faced with the choice between betraying my country or my friends, I hope I would have the courage to betray my country." Few would be convinced by his argument.

Anthony Blunt and the Homintern

Both Anthony Blunt and Guy Burgess, two of the five spies, were homosexual, while another Maclean, was bisexual. My father told me that the Service had an unofficial way of referring to this group who all spied for the Communist Party. The Comintern was the abbreviation for the Communist International: the group which set itself up to try to bring about a world-wide communist government. So to the Security Service, the five men were known unofficially as the Homintern! NR

My father continued: "And of course Anthony Blunt was in the office during the War, and none of us thought that he was ever likely to be a spy." (*NR: "Completely the wrong type, wasn't he?"*) "Absolutely, and immediately Burgess and Maclean disappeared, he offered to let us into their flat to search around and find anything. We didn't know, of course, that he had already been there, and removed anything which might be likely to give them away. But there are some things he didn't remove, which acted as the basis for a very large investigation which we carried out, about people who were cooperating with Burgess. One of them was a man who still lives in France, who was revealed as the fourth or fifth man, John Cairncross. All sorts of people tried to guess who this man was, until eventually a Russian defector from the Russian Embassy here, gave us proof that he was the third man or the fourth man."

It is curious Ronnie refers to him as the "third or fourth man", rather than the fourth or fifth. It seems Ronnie regarded Philby as the third man, Cairncross as the fourth man, and thought of Blunt as fifth, because he was less important as a spy, and had stopped his activities after the War. But in the press, Cairncross was talked of as the fifth man, because he was revealed after all the others, including Blunt.

[*NR: "What about Blunt, and how he was treated? Do you think he was rather lucky?"*]

"Well, no, because Blunt had determined that he would never tell, and there was nobody who could tell on him. It was only when he got absolute assurance that he would not be prosecuted, that he decided he would say something about it."

There have been several TV dramas about the Cambridge Spies. One, broadcast in 1987, starred Ian Richardson as Blunt, and also brought in another character, the MP Goronwy Rees. In a deathbed confession Rees said that Burgess had approached him before the War and invited Rees to join him in spying for Russia. Rees refused, but felt he should not betray a confidence by revealing this fact to the authorities.

More recently, there was a four-part BBC TV drama called *Cambridge Spies*, shown in 2003. This starred Samuel West as Blunt and Toby

From *Blunt – the Fourth Man*, a BBC drama broadcast in 1987, starring Anthony Hopkins as Burgess (left), Ian Richardson as Blunt (centre) and Michael Williams (late husband of Judi Dench) as Goronwy Rees MP.

Stephens as Philby. Most recent is the exciting and well-written novel, *The Trinity Six*, by Charles Cumming, published in 2011. The plot imagines that there was a sixth spy, and that his existence was covered up by the security services.

Ironically, one Russian defector could have prevented any of the Cambridge spies retaining any credence or influence from 1945 onwards. In September 1945 Konstantin Volkov, from the Russian Secret Service, had offered to defect to Britain. He offered the names of some Soviet agents, including, he said, more than one Soviet agent working on British soil, who was very senior in MI6. It was Kim Philby who made contact with him and arranged to meet him in Istanbul. In fact, Philby tipped off the Russians immediately, then delayed his trip by several days. During that time, of course, Volkov was kidnapped by the Russians, tortured, then bundled on a plane and taken back to Russia, where he was shot. Philby's description of Volkov as a "nasty piece of work" makes a much better description when applied to Philby himself, in arranging for the liquidation of Volkov. When I discussed Volkov with my father, I remember how much he regretted what had happened. If Philby had not been in that senior position, and arranged that, then all the important traitors in our Secret Service would have been exposed in 1945. In that case, it is likely that few, if any, of the traitors would have still been active during the Cold War.

Jenifer Hart

Having discussed all these spies, and their successful infiltration of the Foreign Office and Security Service, one might have thought that any civil servant who was in the same department would have been removed or given other duties. Then others, perhaps more aware of the dangers, could have taken over. The more so with my father, who, after all, said he was in charge of the investigations of the various spies discussed above. However, he proved to be aware of one spy, or potential spy, when others were not willing to believe it.

Jenifer Hart's rather suitably entitled *"Ask Me No More"*. Was she worried that, if interrogated, she might give away too much?

Jenifer Hart was the wife of Professor HLA Hart, Professor of Jurisprudence at Oxford. He had been at Bletchley Park during the War. He knew that his wife was more left-wing than him, but thought little more about it. What he did not know was that she had joined the Communist Party in 1935, and stayed a member of it, even when she joined the Civil Service.

Her husband eventually became Principal of Brasenose College, Oxford, while she obtained a lectureship in history at St Anne's College. During the 1980s, she admitted she had been a communist, but said that, although she did not declare her membership, she never passed over any information to the Soviets, despite her holding a job which could have given the Russians extremely useful information. Anyway, she says in her autobiography that in 1966 she was contacted by MI5, and agreed to be interviewed by Peter Wright and another man – who is likely to be my father. She says that after the interview she was never again asked to serve on the Civil Service Final Selection Board. And when both Chapman Pincher and Nigel West implied she had given away secrets, she decided not to sue them for libel.

It is said that my father spotted the danger of this at a time when few of his contemporaries thought it likely. So, though he, like all his fellow officers, was unaware of the treachery of people like Philby, his spotting Jenifer as a possible spy led to him being retained in The Office.

EIGHTEEN

THREE YEARS IN NEW ZEALAND

IN 1957 THE family went out to New Zealand. As Ronnie said in his interview, "(the Office) decided that, having had so much counter-espionage experience, I could help in New Zealand. And so Mary and I went to New Zealand from 1957 to 1960 to help run the counter-espionage section there." In fact, Mary told me later, he went out there to supervise setting up the New Zealand MI5. Since MI5 had its staff in Britain, but Ronnie was being sent aboard, he was therefore seconded to the Foreign Office for this three year posting.

We went out by boat, the Rangitata, and came back by another, the Strathmore. In 1957 and '60 the standard way to travel abroad was still by ship: flying was far too expensive, even for government officials. We went out via the Panama Canal, and came back via the Suez Canal. So, in the course of those three years, we circumnavigated the globe. On the way out, in the Pacific, our boat moored off Pitcairn Island about 4 am in the morning, and some of its inhabitants came out to the ship to sell us wooden sculptures they had made.

Mr. R. T. Reed,

Office of the United Kingdom.
High Commissioner.
Wellington.

Left: a photo of Ronnie from 1959, with *above*, his business card.

Officially First Secretary at the British High Commission, Ronnie was actually setting up a New Zealand MI5. Up to that point, it had been run as a colonial venture from back in London. One might wonder how many spies were actually based out in New Zealand. But what you have to remember is that most countries send out, in their embassies, people who try to find out information which their own government would like to know about the country. So we needed branches of MI5 in most of the colonies, so that foreigners could not carry out their dastardly spying activities! After setting it up, he left it in the hands of a man called Bill Gilbert, who was the first Head of MI5 in New Zealand.

Talking of colonialism in New Zealand in the late 1950s, I do remember that, to hear the general news, we switched on our wireless set, and found the sound of "Lilli Bolero". That was the signature tune of the BBC's World Service. We then listened to the World Service, giving us the news, broadcast direct from London! Because it was travelling 12,000 miles, I knew Lilli Bolero in a very distorted version, and only found out what it really sounded like, when I came back to England. On some days radio reception of the news from London was so poor that the New Zealand Broadcasting Service had to use a recording they had made some hours earlier, or even the previous day. There were local broadcasting stations, but they just put out pop music and entertainment: the News came from London. And indeed, New Zealand did not get television until about 1976, just forty years after we had it in England. That might have originated Clement Freud's observation, that he had visited New Zealand once, but found it was closed. Certainly, we came across more than one café which always closed for lunch!

In those days, the country was big on Do-it-Yourself, but doing it yourself was often accompanied by the expression "She'll be Right" meaning the botched job should be OK. It often was not, so in school we had to write Moral Tales on how "She'll be Right" could bring disaster.

All dressed up with somewhere to go: my parents in full fig for a Government reception. Note my mother's fur wrap: very politically incorrect these days!

As the most common hobby was being outside and Doing it Yourself, the country was very short of culture. My mother used to quote the fact that while we were there, there was just one cinema and one theatre in the capital city, Wellington. But they did have distinguished visiting artists. One of those was the violinist David Oistrakh, whose example inspired my brother Adrian (named after the conductor Sir Adrian Boult) to become a professional violinist. In 2011 he celebrated his 40th year playing in Covent Garden Orchestra.

Out in New Zealand, my father worked in Wellington, the capital city. Many of those who worked there, lived, as we did, at the other end of the Bay, in Lower Hutt (on the Hutt River). We lived, first, at 11 Rangiora Street, which was still there when my brother visited it in 2005. We were then moved to 70 Kings Crescent, a very grand house which has since been demolished. It was previously lived in by the sister of Michael Miles, a TV personality, whose catchphrase was "your quiz and quizzitor", and who is best remembered now for the ITV quiz show *Take Your Pick*. Michael Miles did indeed visit the house while we were there.

One of the Reeds' main duties in New Zealand was to wine and dine the great and the good at our government-provided home. There my parents gave cocktail parties, at least once a month. Among the grand fare paid for by the High Commission was oysters: my first taste of them. There were two sorts: the larger special oysters, and the more common Rock Oysters: both types local to New Zealand. After we returned to Britain in 1960, my next sight of an oyster was in 1974, when some were being sold from a stall at Southampton for 50p each. I splashed out on three for 50p each, just to reacquaint myself with the taste!

Government House, Wellington, NZ.
It was completed in 1910.

There were also Garden Parties given at Government House. At one such party the special visiting guest was the Queen Mother. My mother remembered that when HRH came up to the group which included my mother, she showed a broad smile, which won everyone over. By contrast, Mary was quite shocked at some of the racism espoused by those who should have known better. When she was discussing the native Maoris with a fellow diplomat, she was surprised to hear him say, "Ah, but you wouldn't want your daughter to marry one of them, would you?" My parents thought colour had no importance, and Mary said to myself and my brother they would have no objections whatever, if one of us wanted to marry someone who was coloured.

Since my father was a Senior Officer in the Security Service, his duties often led him to visit islands in the Pacific which belonged to the British Commonwealth, and he always sent back a postcard. He visited Fiji several times. It may have been these experiences which made him take a particular interest in the series of radio talks called *A Pattern of Islands*, by Arthur Grimble, on which his book of the same name was based. Grimble was a British Colonial Commissioner in the Gilbert and Ellice Islands. Taking a particular interest in the traditions of the native people, he showed considerable initiative by learning Gilbertese. I remember these popular talks arousing the same kind of fascination which one now expects from a documentary by David Attenborough.

Ronnie's QSL card for his NZ address – the card he would send to other radio hams after talking to them. Note the kiwi and palm tree!

Ronnie kept up his amateur radio interests while we were in the country, and duly had a new QSL card. His call sign now changed from G2RX to ZL2RT. This was made up of ZL for New Zealand: the 2 from his British call-sign, and RT from Ronald Thomas. Among those he called up were his amateur radio friends back in England. I remember his amusement when he was talking to someone in Herne Hill, SE London, and they said they were on quite a high hill: 100 feet! Around the Bay of Wellington, where we lived, the hills were at least 1000 feet in height.

We went on holiday for the allowed leave period of three weeks each year. This was enjoyable, but had problems. Our car pulled a large caravan behind it, in which we slept overnight. But all the roads at that time were dirt roads: the only tarmac was in cities. Thus, whenever we arrived at our stop for the night, we would open the door of the caravan to find a really thick layer of dirt had made its way inside, built up from driving during the day. So before we could do anything, all the surfaces had to be swept and wiped down.

Lake Waikaremoana, with some of the dramatic hills surrounding it.

On one occasion we travelled 80 miles to reach Lake Waikaremoana, a scenic lake deep in the mountains. Almost all the journey was on winding roads along the sides of mountains, with a deep precipice on one side. And the thick forest, or "bush" as it was called, prevented one seeing any of the views one might have expected. As the roads were dirt and gravel roads, that cut our speed right down to about 15 mph, to avoid us sliding off the edge. Little wonder that, by the time we finally got there, my young brother and I were crying with boredom. We then found that the "scenic lake" had largely dried up, with acres of dried mud round its edges. Still, perhaps you could call it an adventure. Fifty years on, the Lake is probably transformed.

My father had bought a colour slide camera, so as we visited the tourist attractions of the country in the late 1950s, he took over 100 colour photos of these locations, and carefully labelled each one. Despite the occasional down-side, most of the sights were enjoyable, some spectacular, and often very beautiful.

Arrowtown "Post and Telegraph" office, now run by the local museum. Note the hitching post for your horse!

I remember us visiting Arrowtown, for example, in the South Island. Arrowtown had been a gold rush town, like those in the Wild West. It was now completely deserted. In the main street, one could see the shops advertising what they had sold: the buildings surviving like ghosts. Many of its inhabitants had chosen to live in old railway cars, which were still left there on the hillside. Fifty years on, the town is now a flourishing and well populated tourist attraction.

The Franz Joseph Glacier.

One fascinating experience was the hot springs and geysers of Rotorua: exciting in themselves. But the most dramatic experience was when we went walking, with a guide, on the ice of the Franz Joseph Glacier, on the west coast of the South Island. The surface is nothing like as smooth as one would think from aerial photographs, and the guide had to chop steps in the mounds of ice, to create a path, often with a crevasse beside us to keep us on our toes. Exciting, but with a distinct tinge of danger! I was pleased to hear that Health and Safety has not yet banned such expeditions for the adventurous. When we went to the Deep South of the South Island we visited Invercargill. So often, one finds Scottish names transferred to New Zealand, and indeed the countryside is really more like Scotland than anywhere (give or take the hot springs of Rotorua). In Invercargill, we were shown what looked like a front lawn, and we told that, in winter, that was the skating rink. The winter down there was so cold that one simply had to pour water on the lawn to create the rink. By contrast, the original capital, Auckland, near the north end of the North Island, was almost mediterranean, with tropical palms lining many of the streets. So New Zealand really is a country of contrasts. But that's not surprising when it stretches over 1000 miles from north to south.

The magnificent façade of the Grand Hotel in Auckland. Dating from 1889, the façade is now dominated by the office building into which it was incorporated.

Indeed, it was Auckland from which we set off by boat in 1960, to return to Britain. As I remember it, we were flown north from Wellington to Auckland, but from there we made the rest of the journey to England by boat. When we arrived in Auckland, we were accommodated in the largest hotel, the Grand Hotel, in Princes Street. My father remembered it well. As they had been packing the day before, my parents were tired, and hung the Please Do Not Disturb sign on the hotel room door. The following morning, promptly at seven o'clock, the New Zealand chambermaid walked in the room and said, "You didn't mean this notice, did you?" They said, "Well, we did actually." "Ah well, I've brought your tea." "OK. We'll have it then." "Do you take sugar?" "No, thank you." "Oh well, don't stir it then."

Among the guests who had stayed there were Noel Coward, Margot Fonteyn and Lord Montgomery. But perhaps my parents' experience was a sign of the times. The building closed as a hotel just six years later, in 1966. The vaulted ceilings and ornate mantelpieces are no more, but the façade survives. Incidentally, for those who like art deco architecture, New Zealand can boast a whole city of it: in 1931 the town of Napier was virtually destroyed by an earthquake, which was 7.8 on the Richter scale. It was rebuilt at the height of the Art Deco period. (For comparison, the Christchurch earthquake in 2010 was 7.1 on the Richter scale.)

I have described New Zealand as backward in some ways fifty years ago. But in one respect, politics, it has always led the way. New Zealand was the first country in the world to give all the adult women the right to vote, in 1893.

And in 2005 it became the only country in the world in which all the highest State positions were held by women: Head of State, Governor-General, Prime Minister, Speaker and the Chief Justice.

On the journey back, we stopped at Singapore, where I first saw policemen with guns in their holsters. Then through the Suez Canal, and eventually as far as Marseilles. As we were by the harbourside, my father was very keen to try a local delicacy: bouillabaisse – the fish soup of the region. We sat at a table on the dockside and tried it: it was delicious. We finally got back to England, and, from the ship, found ourselves looking out, not at the familiar sights of London, but at the docks of Tilbury. Freight, and passenger liners, were already landing people there, rather than London itself.

NINETEEN

RONNIE AT HOME AND WORK, 1960-1976

ON OUR FAMILY'S return in 1960, we were accommodated for a short time in a government flat in central London, at North Audley Street, while looking to buy a home. The building was owned by the Security Service, and in the flat above us was Ronnie's old colleague Jim Skardon. We visited Jim in his flat a couple of times, and he showed me his large stamp collection. He had some unusual stamps, as he had been abroad to many Commonwealth countries for work, and I admired several of them. He then asked me if I was really keen on collecting stamps. At that time I still was, and said so. He then said, "Well in that case, if you like, I shall give you my stamp collection." I said I was thrilled, and thanked him profusely. I still keep it carefully. But I added to it, the stamps from the many postcards which Ronnie sent, also from far-flung locations. So the whole is quite an unusual collection.

Ronnie's salary in New Zealand had enabled him to save enough to put down a deposit for a mortgage. For several months the family rented a house in Selby Road, Penge, while they were house-hunting. Ronnie and Mary were eager to buy one of the new 1960s homes then being built by Wates in Farquhar Road, near Crystal Palace. The new ones were all smooth lines, no trouble to dust, and no unnecessary ornament, just like the Swedish houses after which they were modelled. As new properties, these were selling for £5,800 each, but unfortunately, this was more than the Reeds could afford. They were therefore forced to consider an old-fashioned Edwardian property, 2 Court Lane Gardens, off Court Lane in Dulwich, backing on to Dulwich Park. This still had an Aga in the kitchen, stained glass in the front door, decorative woodwork in the hall, and all the other "hideous" Edwardian attributes that any forward-thinking couple hated to live with. However, this property was available for just £4,500. They pointed out to the owner the many disadvantages of this old property, and beat the price down to £4,250. We moved in, late in 1960. When the house finally came to be sold again, in 1995, we observed that the Wates property they had coveted was now worth about half the value of the Court Lane Gardens houses: about £400,000 for the latter. So greatly have the criteria of 'desirable attributes' changed since the 1960s!

The Reeds standing on the patio at the back of the Dulwich house. Taken in about 1965, this photo shows Ronnie (*left*), Nicholas with Tonga the cat (*centre*) and Adrian (*right*). Adrian and I are wearing our Alleyns School ties and blazers.

From 1960 Ronnie used to commute from Herne Hill Station to Victoria Station, from which he travelled to Leconfield House in Curzon Street, where the Office was. Every morning he had a twenty minute walk from his home in Dulwich to the Station, and twenty minutes back in the evening. This regular walk, until he was 60, must have helped to keep him very fit right until his late 70s.

In The Office was a mixture of people, and he told me one anecdote which he said was based on a true story. It concerned a Pole, who was involved in decoding. The Poles were in fact immensely important in the solution which enabled us to read German coded signals. This particular man was brilliant at cryptography, but had very poor basic English. So every lunchtime he would go up to the canteen, and say, in a thick Polish accent, the only thing he knew: "Roast beef, apple pie." After weeks of this unending diet at lunchtime, he spoke to a colleague, who sympathised, and carefully taught him to say, "Ham salad, jam sponge." Next lunchtime, the Pole

Mary on the patio at Dulwich, complete with cigarette and cup of coffee. The cat sitting in the shrubbery was called Tonga. He had turned up, very friendly, in 1956. Queen Salote of Tonga had been the friendliest of the foreign monarchs who came to the Coronation in 1953, so we named the cat after her.

went up to the counter at the canteen. "Ham salad, jam sponge." The waitress replied, "Doyouwantanymayonnaiseonyoursalad?" He tried again. "Ham salad, jam sponge." "Yup," she said. "Doyouwantanymayonnaiseonyoursalad?" He sighed deeply. "OK. Roast beef, apple pie."

Here we can continue my interview with Ronnie.

"When we came back in 1960, I went back to the technical side and travelled round the world, to Africa and the Far East and India, giving advice to people on the sort of equipment they should use. (*NR: "Would this be for transmitting or ?..."*) "No. This was for their own investigations in their own countries. That has all ended now. It was in the colonial era, where we used to advise the Special Branches and the Chiefs of Police. (*This would have to be for things like bugging telephones, or something like that?*) That's right. (*For people who were suspected of subversion.*) That's right, or people who were thought to be engaged in espionage for the Russians, or the Poles, or for Eastern Europe. Of course, when that all came to an end, everything turned over to the IRA."

Mrs (now Dame) Stella Rimington with her first book Open Secret, in which she put MI5 into the public domain, and explained clearly what the Service is for.

During his retirement, Ronnie used to attend occasional meetings or dinners to which present or former members of the Security Service were invited. On one occasion, he attended a dinner addressed by Stella Rimington, who was the first woman Head of MI5, from 1992-96. She spoke about the task of infiltrating the IRA, to try to get advance notice of where they were planning to let off bombs. Up till the 1990s, the only people who were given the task of trying to infiltrate the IRA were police detectives. They were not very effective. To infiltrate the IRA successfully, you had to have the type of devious person who could really convince the IRA they were part of their movement and believed in their policies. While Kenneth Baker was Home Secretary, Mrs Rimington had several times made a presentation to him, trying to get him to agree to MI5 using their agents to infiltrate the IRA. Mr Baker had smiled, and smiled, but absolutely refused to change the policy. (As another politician said, it would probably take major surgery to remove Mr Baker's smile.) But as soon as Baker had gone, and Kenneth Clarke had taken over, in April

1992, she had made the presentation again, and this time Clarke had agreed. What exactly happened after that has not been revealed, but perhaps it is not just coincidence that within five years of the change of policy, the Good Friday Agreement had been signed.

My father continued: "There was a lot of subversion in this country at that time. There were an enormous number of organisations who were, as many of us were, against the Vietnam War, and who were trying to overthrow the Government. It was really quite ludicrous to see the way these people behaved, saying they would stop the Vietnam War. An absolute group of rabble rousers around the American Embassy, when you had the whole panoply of the British Government and the armed forces, who were supporting the Americans." Here one can see my father's automatic support for the establishment, dismissing those who were campaigning against the Vietnam War as being "ludicrous". In fact, if there had not been all those demonstrations in 1968, both here and in America, the Americans might still be in Vietnam now!

"But", said my father, "Many people who played a prominent part in that in 1968, became famous, like Tariq Ali." (*NR: "Well, he's still going as a journalist."*) "He's still going as a journalist, and a very respectable and good journalist too. Jack Straw was also heavily involved, but a perfectly respectable citizen. We didn't investigate them as such, but we kept an eye on their activities. What was particularly interesting was that we managed to infiltrate… I used to go to some of their meetings, and wave the flag and say "Up the anti-Vietnam Group" etc. This was terribly amusing, because the final demonstration to Grosvenor Square was led by one of the Chief Superintendents of Special Branch, and they didn't know it. So we were in complete control of the whole thing. But nobody went to prison unnecessarily. Nobody was investigated unnecessarily, and the whole thing was under control. "

This revelation by my father, of the final demonstration being led by a Chief Superintendent, just shows that infiltration of "subversive" organisations continued after the War. Indeed, it is vital if anti-democratic or violent groups are going to be thwarted by the state.

I decided to try to check my father's statement with Tariq Ali himself, and wrote to him in 2008. Ali had a distinguished Oxford career, and was President of the Oxford Union the year before he went down in 1966.

He replied, "As far as the last Grosvenor Square demo is concerned, it was a Maoist breakaway on October 27th 1968. On behalf of the Vietnam Solidarity Campaign, I had asked for a show of strength on that day, and not a test of strength. For weeks previously the Govt. had spread black propaganda: violence was being planned, the MOD might be attacked and occupied, etc. A tiny Maoist group, probably led by

Tariq Ali and Vanessa Redgrave near Grosvenor Square, seat of the American Embassy, during the demonstrations of 1968.

the Chief Inspector, went to Grosvenor Square, engaged in a tiny punch-up, and ended up playing football with the cops. It did, even at the time, seem like a provocation." So Ronnie's story makes good sense. It would be just this sort of Maoist group which the authorities would regard as most dangerous, in the way Tariq Ali describes, and therefore worth infiltrating.

I went on to ask my father about the National Council for Civil Liberties. (*NR: "The controversial one is supposed to be people like the NCCL."*) "Never did anything about them. We looked to see if they were infiltrated by communists. I co-operated with someone – I won't mention his name – who was on the National Council for Civil Liberties, and asked him why he was still a member, because it seemed to me extremely left wing and anti-government. He said he knew that, but he wanted to change it from inside, and if he was outside he couldn't do anything about it. So he was very helpful."

My father told me that he was also involved in following the police investigations of the Angry Brigade. Little remembered now, the Angry Brigade carried out a string of bomb attacks on government buildings, embassies, corporations and the homes of ministers in the early 1970s. No one was killed. Eight political activists were charged. Five were convicted of conspiracy, and sentenced to up to ten years imprisonment. One of those convicted, John Barker, said later, 'In 1971-72, I was convicted in the Angry Brigade trial and spent seven years in jail. In my case, the police framed a guilty man.'

Tariq Ali himself remembers being approached by someone who was claiming to represent the Angry Brigade, and suggested it might be an idea to plant a bomb at the American Embassy in Grosvenor Square. 'I told them it was a terrible idea. They were a distraction. It was difficult enough building an anti-war movement without the press linking this kind of action to the wider Left.'

While he was still at work, life at home had to take account of Ronnie's need for sleep, so as to be fresh the next day. By contrast, my mother suffered from frequent insomnia, and used to listen to the wireless with headphones during the night. The World Service used to repeat episodes of The Goon Show, and this affected Ronnie, because Mary used to shake with laughter while listening to them, and this woke Ronnie up! No doubt they reached a compromise.

A photo taken in 1973. Ronnie holds their Siamese cat Willow. Mary holds her first grandchild Jacob. Nicholas stands at the back.

They also used to love cats, which tended to be Siamese or, later, Burmese. Their favourite cat in the 1970s was Willow, a blue Siamese. He was a very talkative cat, and particularly so when he came up to my parents' bedroom at night, and meowed his way under the covers. The trouble was that Ronnie needed a good night's sleep, and got fed up with being woken up by the noise. When that happened, he would take Willow downstairs and lock him in the kitchen. Willow fairly rapidly learned that, if he was going to be allowed in the Reeds' bed, he would have to creep up very quietly!

As a regular daily paper, they used to take the *News Chronicle*. When that folded, they moved to *The Times*. They told me that they would have preferred to take *The Independent*, as that was not so wedded to the Conservatives. But they so much enjoyed reading Miles Kington's humorous columns that they stuck to *The Times*. Then, a few years later, Miles moved from *The Times* to *The Independent*. My parents immediately changed their daily paper, to follow him.

It was Miles Kington who told a remarkable story of the 18th century. During the wars against Napoleon, the French sailors had a very effective war-cry. Their first cry was "To the water!", which in French is "A l'eau!" Their second cry was "It is time!" which in French is "C'est l'heure!" So when they encountered the English navy, their war-cry was "A l'eau, c'est l'heure!" In English, this sounds remarkably like "'Allo, sailor!"

Kington invented the term Franglais and wrote whole books about the mixture of French and English. But he could also do it in Latin. When the Pope suggested that Latin might become the European language, Kington came up with some helpful translations, e.g. Quid pro quo: the sterling exchange rate; Adsum: small extras on the bill; Infra dig: terrible accommodation.

Ronnie, like Miles Kington, was a great admirer of the plays of Tom Stoppard. When he went to see Stoppard's *Jumpers*, he was sure that the part of the philosophy professor (played by Nigel Hawthorne) was based on the Oxford philosopher Freddie Ayer. My father met him, and Hugh Trevor-Roper, another Oxford professor, during the War, where both were in intelligence.

Victor Rothschild: the 3rd Baron Rothschild.

Another person my father worked with, both during the War and after it, was Lord Rothschild. He was the MI5 expert on explosives, and he used to have long conversations with Eddie Chapman about the best way to blow up a safe. At the end of the War, according to my father, one of those who said he was going to vote Labour was Lord

Rothschild. The Americans, with whom my father was working, were absolutely astonished when they heard this. After all, an English Lord was part of the Establishment: it made no sense to them that he should vote Labour. But Rothschild's vote in 1945 was in fact indicative of how most of the country felt. It is still very remarkable how massive Labour's majority was in 1945. But at the time, the majority of the country had become convinced there should be a "bright new dawn" after the war, and the man who had brilliantly won an aggressive war was not the right man to lead radical reform in peacetime. In 1945 people like Rothschild were also impressed by the idea of a National Health Service, which had been proposed by Beveridge and widely discussed during the War.

Harold Macmillan, around the time he was Prime Minister, from 1957-63.

Talking of Lords, my father was well aware of one. When I was walking with him once in central London in the 1960s, we spotted a Rolls Royce, he said, "Look at that car: we might see someone interesting get into it." And a moment later, we did: it was the then Duke of Bedford, very recognisable, and the letters on his car number plate, which my father had spotted, were DOB.

On another occasion, he told me, he was just outside Victoria Station, at the pedestrian crossing (now a light-controlled crossing) which led across to the small clock-tower Little Ben. Coming up to the crossing, walking extremely slowly, was an elderly gentleman with a moustache, whom my father recognised immediately. Ronnie said, "You're not used to walking. You're used to travelling in a Rolls Royce." And a very cultured voice in rich tones replied, "I've never had a Rolls Royce. I once had a Humber!" It was Harold MacMillan, and the Humber was indeed his vehicle of choice.

Ronnie told me that he spent his last few years at the Office dealing with personal security matters, such as the latest devices for ensuring the security of documents in suitcases. In 1976 he retired at 60, which was then the standard retirement age for civil servants. He was worried about getting bored in retirement, and enquired about the possibility of continuing at The Office part-time. However, he finally decided to retire completely, and, as he said later, had never been as busy as when he retired!

TWENTY

R.V. JONES

IN 1977 MY FATHER and I were both watching a BBC TV series called "The Secret War". The main interviewee in it was Professor R.V. Jones, who was by this time Professor of Natural Philosophy (i.e. Physics) at Aberdeen University. He, as a young scientist during the War, had discovered that the Germans had invented a form of electronic beam, along which attacking Germans planes could fly, to direct them to their target. Having discovered its existence, Jones then invented a way of either jamming the beam, or deflecting it, to make it ineffective, in what became known as the "Battle of the Beams". He then received intelligence which made him think the Germans had invented some kind of rocket. But he was up against scientists who argued that, since we had tried to make a rocket and failed, there was simply no way the Germans could have made a successful one. He continued to argue his point cogently, until his proof arrived just after D-Day, with a big bang, in the shape of the V-2 itself.

R.V. Jones, at the time of his TV series.

Jones wrote a book on his wartime work, entitled *Most Secret War – British Scientific Intelligence 1939-45* (1978) which told the complete tale, and which A.J.P. Taylor described as "the most fascinating book on the Second World War that I have ever read". (It was reissued by Penguin in 2009.) Thirty years on, one can probably still agree with Taylor's judgement.

When I discussed Jones with my father, he agreed it was a fascinating story. His only slight doubt was to wonder whether, in fact, Jones had always been right about everything during the War! But then, my father did not mention any mistakes he made during the war. For example, the occasion when he was supervising Eddie Chapman, and the two of them forgot to include the special code letters, which implied "this message is genuine". Without those letters, which they had omitted, the implication was "I have been captured, and this message is being transmitted to mislead you." Both men were in deep trouble when they allowed that to happen. However, Eddie said in his next message, "Sorry I forgot the code letters", and the Germans did not raise a query. In Jones's book, and my father's interview, it's your opportunity to explain and excuse: you leave it to others to criticise you!

Jones went to Alleyn's School, one of what were then two boys' schools set up under the Foundation established by the Shakespearian actor Edward Alleyn. The other was Dulwich College. There was a friendly rivalry between the two schools, with the College producing more Oxbridge entrants and famous "sons". But it was Alleyn's School whose English master founded the National Youth Theatre, which included two former Alleyn's pupils, Julian Glover and Simon Ward.

While Alleyn's was a Direct Grant School, Dulwich College was a Public School. Ludovic Kennedy was once chairing a debate on the Pros and Cons of Public School education. He started by saying, "As your impartial Chairman in this debate, I ought to declare that I have an interest, because I went to Eton. But that does not necessarily mean that I believe *all* Public Schools should be abolished."

As an Alleyn Old Boy, Jones returned more than once for Prize-Giving Day, when he would give out the prizes and make a speech.

My father attended the prize-giving at the School in 1965, and obviously remembered his speech. He therefore wrote to him in 1981 and probably expressed his appreciation of the TV series. R.V. Jones replied, "Thank you for your letter of 3rd July. It happens that I do still have copies of the Prize-giving Address that I gave at Alleyn's in 1965,

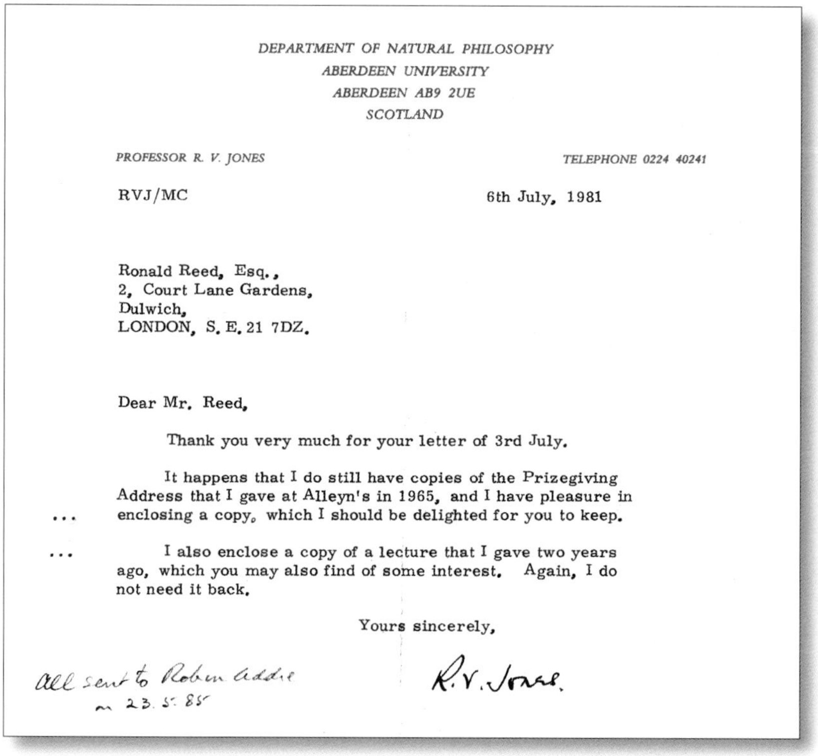

DEPARTMENT OF NATURAL PHILOSOPHY
ABERDEEN UNIVERSITY
ABERDEEN AB9 2UE
SCOTLAND

PROFESSOR R. V. JONES

TELEPHONE 0224 40241

RVJ/MC

6th July, 1981

Ronald Reed, Esq.,
2, Court Lane Gardens,
Dulwich,
LONDON, S.E.21 7DZ.

Dear Mr. Reed,

Thank you very much for your letter of 3rd July.

It happens that I do still have copies of the Prizegiving Address that I gave at Alleyn's in 1965, and I have pleasure in enclosing a copy, which I should be delighted for you to keep.

I also enclose a copy of a lecture that I gave two years ago, which you may also find of some interest. Again, I do not need it back.

Yours sincerely,

R.V. Jones.

All sent to Robin Addie on 23.5.85

Jones's letter to my father. Ronnie lent the letter and enclosures to Robin Addie, who it seems was another radio ham, had been based at Bletchley Park, and published an article with his memories of Alan Turing.

and I have pleasure in enclosing a copy, which I should be delighted for you to keep. I also enclose a copy of a lecture that I gave two years ago, which you may also find of some interest. Again, I do not need it back. Yours sincerely, R.V. Jones."

The speech he gave to the School in 1965 talked partly about the teachers he remembered, and some of that appears briefly in his book. But he also gave an interesting example of the scientific method. "It concerns a scientist who had reached the stage in his career when he earned enough to be able to sample for the first time the pleasure of the world. Among these pleasures was alcohol, and he decided he must learn to drink. He therefore undertook a series of experiments in which he drank on successive evenings first whisky and soda, then brandy and soda, and finally rum and soda. On each morning afterwards he woke up with a headache. Then, applying scientific method as expounded by Francis Bacon, he looked for the common factor as the explanation of his headaches. As a result, he gave up drinking soda water."

He went on to say that an eminent scientist had once been giving an after-dinner speech at which the host was the Crown Prince of Sweden. The scientist told this joke, and was surprised that everyone fell about laughing, even more than he might have expected. When things quietened down, he noticed that the Crown Prince was drinking soda-water. What he did not realise was that it was common knowledge in Sweden that the Crown Prince had recently been advised by his doctors to refrain from alcohol, and to drink soda-water instead!

Statistics have to be handled with care. One cynic remarked, "A politician uses statistics like a drunk uses a lamp-post: for support, rather than illumination." Perhaps the best example was a man who was intending to travel by air, but was worried by the increasing risk of terrorists taking a bomb onto his plane. He decided to consult a statistician. The statistician thought hard, and came up with some advice. He said, "The chances of a terrorist taking a bomb onto the same plane as yours, are one in 100,000. But the chances of two bombs being taken onto your plane, are one in ten million. So my advice is: take a bomb with you!"

At the school prize-giving in 1965 I was, by some fluke, receiving three prizes, and when I went forward finally, Jones leant forward and said, "What are you planning to study?" I replied, "I hope to be an archaeologist, Sir." At that, I fear there was a distinct look of

Alleyn's School, one of what were then two boys' schools set up under the Foundation established by the Shakespearian actor Edward Alleyn.

disappointment on his face – he probably felt all bright pupils should try to become scientists!

The second article Jones sent to my father was a talk he gave to York University in 1979. In it, he explained why he thought Britain had declined after the War, and how we could improve. Jones also talked about over-manning, and made an interesting prediction. "The latest worry is the "chip" revolution. But if advances in electronics may eliminate jobs which require moderate mental ability, the decline in energy resources such as oil, may put a premium on physical labour." Sadly for the labour force, there is no sign of that, thirty years on. It is far more likely we shall find other types of labour-saving energy to replace what we have at present.

TWENTY-ONE

RONNIE IN RETIREMENT, 1976-95

ONCE RONNIE RETIRED, my parents seriously considered moving back to Hampstead, which they had left in 1952. They had left Hampstead, because the maisonette at Belsize Lane was not suitable for a family with two young children, and the neighbours constantly complained about the noise. So my parents put an advertisement in the Evening Standard, asking to swap their accommodation in Hampstead, with a flat with a garden. They got a reply from a nurse, who lived in a ground floor flat with a garden at 12 Mowbray Road, Upper Norwood, not far from the Crystal Palace. She had been making the long commute every day from Norwood to Hampstead, where she worked at the Royal Free Hospital. So my parents moved to Norwood in 1952, and stayed there till they were posted to New Zealand in 1957.

Twenty years on, they looked at returning to Hampstead, where they kept up with friends, many from the South Place Ethical Society and the Progressive League. One house in Hampstead was similar to their Dulwich one which, at the back, looked out onto Dulwich Park. In Hampstead they saw a very attractive house whose back gate went straight out onto the Heath. They were so impressed they asked the present occupants why they had decided to move. They explained, "Well, it's the burglars. They come straight off the Heath and have burgled us more than once." So, despite the attractions of that house, they decided to give it a miss. Eventually they decided that, as they had made a lot of friends in Dulwich, it might be a mistake to give up all that and move to Hampstead.

In the community in Dulwich, Ronnie became active in the Dulwich Society, and often took charge of the amplification equipment for speakers' voices, if someone came to speak at the Society. More particularly, he was very active on the Trees Sub-Committee of the Dulwich Society, often attending meetings with the Governors or their representatives. He was never willing to be Chairman of it, probably because he was always anxious to keep a low profile in public. This anxiety seems to have been caused by his unwillingness to be questioned by journalists about his experiences in MI5. If asked, he simply pointed out that under the Official Secrets Act, he could say nothing. But we have seen above how he used to attend meetings of an anti-Vietnam group. He was doing so on behalf of The Office, to keep an eye on their activities. To remain incognito at those meetings would mean keeping a low profile in his private life.

Ronnie sitting beside his amateur radio equipment in 1984.

In his retirement, Ronnie enjoyed fixing up things around the house. His wife Mary strained her back in about 1970, and became increasingly unable to stand or do any work. So he ended up largely running the household and the garden. He also enjoyed buying better equipment for his amateur radio, and continued as an amateur radio ham until the month he died. He also bought a Dolby sound system, with which he could enjoy their large collection of long-playing records, and later CDs, of classical music. He had enjoyed singing tenor as an amateur, and had some lessons from Walter Grüner, Professor of Singing at the Guildhall School of Music. So among his LP and CD recordings, pieces for voice and piano featured strongly. He particularly enjoyed the Schubert song cycles sung by Dietrich Fischer-Dieskau, accompanied on the piano by Gerald Moore. Ronnie liked the anecdote told by Gerald Moore, about one occasion when Moore was entering America, carrying with him two of his own books. The first was his autobiography, called *Am I too Loud?* (an accompanist's habitual question). The other was called "The Unashamed Accompanist". The second book, the customs decided, must, from its title, be a pornographic work, and so confiscated it. But then they could see a possible connection with his first book, so that was confiscated as well! One should not digress, but on another occasion the customs officers stopped a vicar, and were searching through his luggage. He asked them what they were looking for, and they explained it was pornography. He replied, "I'm afraid you won't have any luck there: I don't even possess a pornograph."

Ronnie of course also used his sound system for listening to the radio. I well remember his fury when the *Radio Times* which, after all, had started with just the radio programmes, relegated the radio programmes to a separate section at the back of the magazine, thus indicating the low priority they gave to radio, and making those pages difficult to consult. Both Ronnie and I moved our allegiance to the Saturday edition of the *Daily Mail*, in which the radio programmes are listed on the next page to the TV programmes. Ronnie and Mary were very keen on opera, especially Wagner, and was delighted when their second son Adrian became a senior violinist in Covent Garden Orchestra. This sometimes enabled Mary and Ronnie to get seats for an opera when it would have been almost impossible otherwise. As an example of Ronnie's wide knowledge of classical singing, he was once listening to the distinguished musicologist Paul Hamburger talking about classic recordings of French song. Hamburger was playing recordings anonymously, saying that he did not want the name to distract the listener from the point he was making. Playing recordings by a Frenchwoman, Hamburger was saying that she had no idea how to sing French songs. But my father recognised the singer as Dame Maggie Teyte (by whom he had several recordings), and said that he was quite unconvinced by Paul Hamburger's trenchant criticisms.

Gerald Moore (*left*) and Fischer-Dieskau (*above him*) with Elisabeth Schwarzkopf recording songs by Brahms. By coincidence, I met Ronnie at a talk in 1978, where he and Leslie Minchin (from Hampstead) had gone to see Schwarzkopf talking about her career, at the Royal Festival Hall.

At the Progressive League in Hampstead in the 1940s, Ronnie and Mary had met a couple called Leslie Minchin and Celia Fremlin. Celia was a thriller writer, while Leslie was a gas engineer. At that time, they were living in a flat in Parkhill Road, Hampstead, which had been occupied previously by Henry Moore. My parents kept in touch with Leslie and Celia, who, by the 1970s had moved to South Hill Park, also in Hampstead. Around that time, my father went to help Leslie with his TV video-recorder. Both were engineers, of gas and of radio, so it should not have been difficult for them to fix it. However, it was the latest elaborate model. My father said they had spent three hours trying to programme it. Ronnie explained that, when you were following the instructions, you had to carry out each stage in the complicated procedure within ten seconds. If you paused at any point for more than ten seconds, to check what to do next, the machine would go right back to the beginning and you had to start again. The two engineers finally gave up in despair. One can only think the machine had some kind of safety device in mind, and that programming it like that would make the recorder more secure. It did indeed – so secure, it could not be used! Soon afterwards, Leslie had a burglary, and the video-recorder was stolen. After claiming on the insurance, he was very careful to buy the simplest possible recorder to replace the stolen one!

Celia Fremlin, the novelist and thriller-writer, in her Hampstead home with her cat Stripey.

Leslie was quite a keen amateur musician, and he and his wife used to arrange musical soirees in their Hampstead home. This gave an opportunity for Leslie to sing old English folksongs, and sometimes more ambitious pieces by composers like Schubert. Unfortunately, he had a really terrible voice, and one just had to put up with it. However, there were other, sometimes semi-professionals, who put up a good show.

One of those who used to attend was Walter Grüner, who was Professor of Singing at the Guildhall School of Music. (One of his pupils was Patricia Rosario.) He had briefly agreed to teach Leslie singing, but after one lesson, refused to teach him any more. I do remember him being irritated by Leslie singing a song in which he pronounced the word "abend" ("evening") as "aybend". Walter said,

"You are singing German, man. The Word is pronounced "ahbend" not "aybend."

When Walter died, my father knew that he had left money to endow an annual singing competition. My father attended the first such competition, which was said to be organized just as Walter had specified in his Will. For some reason, my father did not take this at face value, and went up to Somerset House in London to look up the Will. But in the Will was recorded, simply Walter's wish for the money to be used for such a competition, with virtually no details about its organisation. Ronnie then contacted the Trustees, only to be told that he was right: the details were not in the Will. Walter had worked them out on paper, but not got round to enshrining them in the Will. This gives some idea of the thoroughness which Ronnie would apply to a subject, once he got the bit between his teeth!

But Ronnie could also be a terrible pessimist. When I produced a book about Pissarro's paintings of South London, and said I was charging £5.50 a copy, he said, "You'll never sell copies at that price." He turned out to be wrong: they all went within a year. But in the Civil Service, at that time, it was far safer to be an pessimist than an optimist. You would then be a regarded as "sound", with no "hair-brained" ideas. And if anything went wrong, the pessimists could always say, "I told you so."

He had long taken an interest in architecture, and, in his later years, invited me to accompany him on a visit to Crossness Power Station, and another on a guided tour of The Paragon in Blackheath. That is a model crescent of houses overlooking the Heath. Partly damaged by the War, the houses were taken over and renovated in the late 1940s, and The Paragon is now comparable only with something like the Royal Crescent in Bath. My parents took an interest when I became the Founder-Chairman of the Friends of Shakespeare's Globe in 1985. But my mother expressed scepticism, as it did seem a weird American idea (from Sam Wanamaker) to reconstruct a building which had entirely disappeared. After it became Southwark's most

The Paragon, Blackheath.

popular tourist attraction, they changed their minds, and often used to take part in the play-readings held at The Globe.

As Ronnie took an interest in the local amenities, he was disappointed when he noticed that, of all the front gardens in Court Lane and Court Lane Gardens, only one was in a mess. It really detracted from the road. It was also unfortunate that the owners happened to be Indian. Eventually, he told me, this couple had received an anonymous letter. It commented on the neglected garden, and went on, "Some people have been remarking that, as you are an Indian couple, perhaps one should expect that. I do not take that view. But it does not help those trying not to be prejudiced, if people see that one garden left in that state by Indian owners. It would therefore be very helpful if the garden could be tidied up, so the wrong inference is not drawn." Ronnie said that within a couple of weeks, their garden looked just as good as the rest. Of course, he could not comment on who might have written the anonymous letter. But it was good to think it had an effect!

My parents on their Ruby Wedding Anniversary in 1986. The party, with all the food coloured ruby red, was organised by my brother and his wife in their garden in Brockley, SE London.

In 1984, Don Cupitt launched a book and a BBC TV series entitled *The Sea of Faith.* The expression comes from Matthew Arnold's famous poem *Dover Beach*, in which the poet laments that belief in the supernatural is ebbing away, like the tide. It is clear my parents were interested in *The Sea of Faith*. As my father said, "It would be nice to think that, when we die, there isn't just nothing afterwards."

In the 1970s, Mary had become a voluntary helper at St. Barnabas Church in Calton Avenue, Dulwich, and was one of those who volunteered to keep it open during the day. She had decided she should give the Church a second try, and became a regular attender

St Barnabas Church in Calton Avenue, Dulwich. This building was sadly destroyed by fire in 1992, two years before its centenary. In the photo, one can make out the white stripes painted round the trees to stop pedestrians bumping into them during the wartime blackout.

at St Barnabas. However, once the vicar changed, and the new one became, as she put it, "all happy clappy", she could not take it, and no longer attended. Once Ronnie retired, the two of them regularly helped in transporting some of the more elderly parishioners to their communal afternoon tea once a week.

Among Ronnie's other interests were local history: he was a long-standing member of the Friends of Nunhead Cemetery, and delivered their Newsletters locally. When I set up the Friends of West Norwood Cemetery in 1988, he immediately joined this group, and gave a donation towards its costs. (He had in fact joined the Cremation Society in the 1930s, when this was still a very radical idea, largely opposed by the established churches.) My father's interest in design was also shown by an unusual remark he made during a meeting of the Friends of (Norwood) Cemetery. The speaker showed a picture of distinctive curtains, and my father said "I think you mean "tart's knickers". He explained the expression arose because the curtains, at the top, go up and down – just like a tart's knickers!

In the autumn of 1994 he was found to have cancer of the oesophagus, which had already spread to the stomach. Its position, near to the spine, made an operation very difficult, so he decided to accept his fate, and died in fact within three months. He died on 22nd January 1995, and an obituary, written anonymously by Nigel West (with some material contributed by myself), was published in the *Daily Telegraph* on the date of his funeral ten days later.

Bill Higman, Chairman of the Dulwich Society, unveiling the tree to Ronnie's memory, at the junction of Turney and Burbage Roads in Dulwich. On the right is the Chairman of the Trees Sub-Committee: Stella Benwell. This ceremony took place in November 1995.

Among those present at the event were Adrian Reed (*centre of group*), Mary Reed (*seated*), and (*at right of group*) two of Adrian's four children, Laura and Samuel.

As a resident of the Borough of Southwark, Ronnie was cremated at Honor Oak Crematorium. Ronnie had expressed a wish to have his ashes scattered in Nunhead Cemetery. However, the Dulwich Society decided to commemorate my father by planting an oak tree in his memory. It stands at the junction of Turney and Burbage Roads in Dulwich. A year after his death, we scattered his ashes around the tree.

TWENTY-TWO

GEORGE BLAKE AND THE "ETHICS" OF SPYING

MY FATHER SAID, "I was therefore in charge of cases like Klaus Fuchs… (etc.), but not George Blake, I'm glad to say."

George Blake is an interesting case. He was prosecuted for betraying secrets, and our agents, to the KGB. Unlike Blunt, he was prosecuted, and in his case, sentenced to 42 years imprisonment. Five years later, he was "sprung" from Wormwood Scrubs Prison, and smuggled to the Soviet Union. Quite a lot of people were sympathetic to those who arranged the escape. After all, he had simply betrayed secrets to the "wrong" side, yet for that, he received far more years of imprisonment than a murderer. The latter might receive a life sentence, but would be likely to be released within 15 to 20 years. Blake was likely to have to serve at least 25 years. Eventually, two of the three people who arranged his escape, Michael Randle and Pat Pottle, decided to reveal how they did it, in a book published in 1989, entitled *The Blake Escape – How we freed George Blake – and Why*. In effect, they were confessing to helping a convicted prisoner escape. So they were prosecuted, in 1991, with the primary evidence being their own account. Both gave well-argued and powerful speeches in defence of their actions. They argued that, although technically they were guilty of the offence they had admitted to, they were morally right to help Blake escape, as his sentence was horrendous and inhuman. Despite the judge instructing the jury to find them guilty, the jury exercised their right to make up their own minds, and found the defendants not guilty.

In my interview with my father, I did not quiz him about George Blake, because I knew that we completely disagreed. He was appalled at what Blake had done, and equally appalled when those who helped him to escape, were found not guilty. I, on the other hand, found it ridiculous that anyone who had betrayed secrets, should be given 42 years in prison. Even at the time, people pointed to the example of Klaus Fuchs. He had given away all the information he had about the West's nuclear research and, as a result, the Russians were able to develop nuclear weapons something like five years earlier than they would have, without Fuchs's help. For such world-changing betrayal, Fuchs was sentenced to just fourteen years. After the trial in 1991, I remember ringing Randle and Potter's solicitor, Benedict Birnberg, to congratulate him on a splendid result. Twenty years on, however, things do not look so clear-cut.

Professor Christopher Andrew is Professor of Modern and Contemporary History at Cambridge University. In 2003, Andrew agreed to become the official historian for the Security Service MI5, and was commissioned to write an official history of the service for their centennial in 2009. He is the only non-member of staff who has been allowed to see all the secret service files. Of course, though allowed to read everything, he has only published the facts which the security service feels can be revealed at this time. In November 2010 he and his fellow historian Peter Hennessy (for whom my father had a great admiration) came to talk about their new books at the Folkestone Books Festival. During the questions, I asked Prof. Andrew about George Blake, and whether the 42 years was justified. I also mentioned the acquittal of Randle and Pottle by their jury. He replied that he too had felt some sympathy towards Blake after the sentence. But then, he said, if you are a spy, and betray the existence of say, 100 spies, to the side which you are supposed to be fighting against, you know that by naming them, they will be arrested by the KGB, tortured, and then executed. In effect, therefore, someone like that is responsible for the murder of 100 people. If faced with such a mass murderer, would you feel that 40 years is too long a sentence? Certainly not. Indeed, if anyone else were responsible for killing, or giving orders for the killing, of 100 people, they would be charged with mass murder, and, if convicted, would never be let out again.

People like Philby and Blake no doubt felt justified in removing those who they knew were actively opposing the communist regime which they supported. And indeed, in time of war, killing 100 people in an opposing army unit might, sometimes, be justified. In times of peace, it seems impossible to justify it.

Interestingly, the press largely seemed to find the jury's verdict perverse, and implied that Pottle and Randle should have been sentenced for their crime. That view was shared by the normally liberal-minded Louis Blom-Cooper QC. One exception, the Guardian, supported the verdict, pointing out that the authorities knew twenty years earlier who had probably helped Blake escape, but chose not to prosecute then. On the other hand, the first time the authorities had proof of their complicity, was when the two published their confession. Should we then accept Professor Andrew's conclusion: that a multiple murderer amply deserves forty years imprisonment?

Why Spy?

Perhaps we should go back to first principles and ask: is spying necessary at all? After all, it was dismissed by Randle and Pottle as a lying and deceitful trade. But they were writing in 1989, before the Berlin Wall fell, and before we found out just how vicious the old USSR could be. Spies have got themselves a bad name. So have politicians. But in the latter case, someone's got to do the job, or we would have no government. But what about spying?

Let us first give it the more neutral term intelligence. It was a lack of intelligence which resulted in nearly 3000 completely innocent people being massacred on 9/11. If intelligence had given some warning, enough to prevent the catastrophe taking place, it would have been immensely valuable. So some intelligence is worthwhile. Indeed, to prevent such mass-murder, it may be essential, as Randle and Pottle concede.

The only way to find out about intended attacks is to infiltrate the gangs who think them up and carry them out. Members of Al Quaeda are not going to steadily defect, one a month, to tell us what they are planning next. Someone needs to infiltrate their movement. To infiltrate successfully, that person has to adopt a completely different character, appearance and mindset. They will say they support the aims of that group, and to do that, they have to lie repeatedly. If they fail to do that, they will not succeed in getting the information, and they will probably be killed by their opponents as well. So spying is necessary, and infiltration inevitably involves deception and lying.

Of course that does not apply to everyone we send abroad. Diplomats were once called "honest men, sent out to lie for their country." That is unfair. Many embassies abroad are staffed by people who spend their time trying, quite legitimately, to obtain greater information about the country in which they are stationed. Spending hours in the library is one way. But if you meet someone from the 'other side' who wants to give you confidential information, you, or a colleague, have to be there to receive it.

George Blake

What about those people who, while being paid by the British to work for the West, are secretly feeding information to the other side – information which, by signing the Official Secrets Act, they have promised, and legally contracted, not to disclose? That is what Philby, Burgess and Maclean did. The last remaining spy still alive who spied for Russia, George Blake, is the one who received the longest sentence. Now aged 89, he is still living in retirement in Moscow. Having written two books on his own life, he is now the subject of a forthcoming biography by Roger Hermiston.

Blake's escape was arranged by Randle and Pottle because they all happened to meet in prison. Randle and Pottle (with others) had been found guilty of conspiracy under the Official Secrets Act. They were sentenced to 18 months imprisonment, because they had conspired to occupy Wethersfield Air Base, on which nuclear weapons were stored. So they found themselves in Wormwood Scrubs prison at the same time as George Blake, with whom they became friends. They were surrounded by other prisoners who all felt, as they did, that 42 years was an outrageous sentence for spying. But after Blake's trial, the press alleged that Blake had given away the identities of at least forty British agents to the Russians. Pottle asked Blake if that was true. He replied that "he had co-operated with the authorities after his arrest, and stressed that there was absolutely no truth in the press rumours that he had been responsible for sending British agents to their deaths." (*The Blake Escape*, p.25) And it seems to be on this assurance that the conspirators decided to try to help him escape. Ten years later, in Blake's own autobiography *No Other Choice* (1990), Blake himself says (pp. 207-8) that, although he had probably identified 400 SIS (MI6) agents to the KGB, he had done so "on the express understanding that they would not come to any harm."As Nigel West puts it, "If he really received such an assurance, it is incredible that he should have believed it." (West, *Seven Spies who Changed the World* (1991), p.144). In an interview after his own book's publication, Blake said, "that he regretted the deaths of the agents he had betrayed." So he knew at that time that some were killed.

Blake then has confessed to giving away to the KGB the names of hundreds of British agents. From what we now know about the USSR in the days of the Cold War, it is impossible to believe that none of them were executed, and far more likely that most of them were. Indeed, from Professor Andrew's reply to my question, it seems that he believes all of them were executed. Professor Andrew's reputation as an historian of intelligence studies was cemented with two studies completed in collaboration with two defectors and former KGB officers, Oleg Gordievsky and Vassili Mitrokhin. The first of these studies was *KGB: The Inside Story*. After working with such people, if anyone should know the fate of traitors to the USSR, it would be Professor Andrew.

But let us, for the moment, give the KGB the benefit of the doubt. Let us take Blake's figure of 400, as roughly the number of agents he betrayed. And let us take the very generous assumption, where the KGB is concerned, that only one in ten of those agents were executed. We come back to the figure of forty agents, for whose deaths Blake was directly responsible. What sentence would be appropriate for that?

There is a special reason why Blake got 42, rather than, say, 40 years. At the time of the trial, 1960, the maximum sentence for one offence under the Official Secrets Act, was 14 years. So Klaus Fuchs got just that. Normally, someone sentenced to three offences would get, say, 14 years, to run concurrently. What was wholly unexpected was the Lord Chief Justice, Lord Parker giving three sentences of 14 years, to run consecutively: a total therefore of 42: the maximum he could give, for the three offences. (Such an unusual judgement did go to appeal, but the appeal was turned down.) Afterwards, it was suggested that the rumoured 40 agents betrayed, neatly equated with the 42 years imposed. The defence barrister at the time, Jeremy Hutchinson, hotly denied (and still denies) that any such calculation was made. But in fact, the judge would have been well aware of these allegations. At the same time, he could not refer to them during the case, primarily because in 1960 the existence of MI6 was still a state secret. If the judge had even mentioned such allegations in court, without them being tested, the defence would have a strong case for appeal against conviction and sentence. Yet it is clear the judge wanted to ensure that Blake would stay behind bars for far longer than one term of fourteen years. Blake's alleged betrayal of agents must have been in the judge's mind.

The question of Blake betraying British agents did come up at least once at the 1991 trial. In his speech at his trial, defending his actions, Dr Michael Randle said the following:

> *George Blake does bear a moral responsibility for the fate of the agents he named to the Soviet Union. But it is clear that his hands would not have been clean if he had continued working faithfully for the British Intelligence Service.*

This excuse, that "they are all as bad as each other", goes along with the view that all spying is wrong. I hope we have seen, that that idea will no longer wash. But there was a vital difference during the Cold War. When people betrayed British agents abroad during the Cold War, it was highly likely they would be executed. During that same Cold War, if we found out about spies working in this country, if they were employed by us, we put them on trial. If they were in an embassy in Britain, we sent them back to their own country. I know of no recorded example (is there one?) during the Cold War, where we either tortured, or executed, a foreigner sent by his masters to spy on us. Removal or imprisonment was the worst punishment.

In 2007 Blake gave a different justification for his actions. He denied being a traitor, insisting that he had never felt British: "To betray, you first have to belong. I never belonged." That may have been how he explained what he did, to himself. But if you feel like that, you do not normally sign the Official Secrets Act and go to work for MI6 with the deliberate intention of undoing as many of their schemes as you can. Nor would you normally betray the existence of hundreds of agents to the other side. It might be said Blake deserved everything he got.

But there is a counter to that, which is also a counter to Professor Andrew's and my father's view. If there is one thing the public knows about spying (from James Bond, if nothing else), it is that the life of a spy is exciting, but it is also dangerous. If you are betrayed by someone on your side, you may be killed by your opponents. You hope not, but there is no guarantee. That is why spies are paid well – they are getting danger money. There is no comparison between arranging the possible death of British agents, to arranging the murder of hundreds of civilians who had no idea they were under threat. There is a difference, but the question remains: how great is that difference?

In this difficult equation, let us throw one more factor into the mix: the British sense of "Fair Play". This is no doubt what motivated the jury into acquitting Randle and Pottle. How is it that Blake got 42 years, while Blunt got off scot free? The point was made more than once by Randle and Pottle. I suggest it had nothing to do with which school or university Blunt and Blake had been to. The difference was that Blake thought we had enough evidence to convict him, and when confronted with it, he made a full confession. In addition, at the trial, he told the judge (through his barrister) that he was proud of what he had done, and had no regrets. If there's one thing likely to make a judge come down hard on you, it is behaviour like that!

In contrast to Blake, the powers that be, never had enough evidence to convict Blunt. Without a confession, there was no case. In Blunt's case, we were so desperate to know what secrets he had given away, that we offered him immunity from prosecution, in exchange for a full confession. He accepted. He then carefully confessed to those offences which he thought (rightly) we probably knew of anyway. Nearly fifty years on, we now realise that he conveniently "forgot" the large amount of other material he had given away. His dedication to the communist cause lasted till the end of his life.

Perhaps the best way of fighting one's way through this minefield of morality, is to draw an analogy with journalism: a profession which competes with spying for the title of the Second Oldest Profession. (We all know what the oldest one is.) If you are a journalist and enter a country from which journalists are banned, you will have an exciting time. If you succeed, you may bring back an important story, and be well paid as well. But if you are caught, for example in Iran or North Korea, you may well be prosecuted for spying, and executed. You take the risk, but you are well aware of the consequences of failure. The same, one could suggest, applies to the profession of spying itself.

The second factor to be borne in mind in discussing the sentences placed on captured agents, is this same "fair play". It seemed a matter of pure chance whether an agent, sentenced to decades in prison, might be swapped with a captured agent from the other side, within a couple of years. After Blake's five years in prison, he had served a longer sentence than most other agents, before they were "exchanged".

Thirdly, what would be the point of locking up Blake for forty years? Once exposed, he could not do the same again. Spies are quite unlike normal criminals who, having served their sentence, come out and may start re-offending. Spies cannot: their cover is blown. Two further points concerning my father. Throughout his life, he was a Labour voter. The only time he wavered, was when the Gang of Four was set up to create the Social Democratic Party, which my parents supported during its existence. But Ronnie always drew a clear distinction between democratic socialism, which he supported, and communism, which he devoted much of his professional life to opposing.

Lastly, when I was having a general discussion with my father about the security services, his reply was interesting. MI5, he said, generally does a good job, and its work is important. As for MI6, he was still not sure whether it had really proved its worth. For someone who must have been collaborating with them at work for decades, that is quite an admission!

None of this should be allowed to detract from the outstanding achievement of our security services during the last War. *The Defence of the Realm: The Authorized History of MI5*, by Professor Christopher Andrew, was published in time for the centenary in 2009. But why was there no exhibition to trumpet our achievements? The Imperial War Museum said they did not have the money. The National Archives said they have enough visitors already. But if necessary, it should be the Security Services themselves who should put on such an exhibition. If public confidence is to be maintained in the Service, they must show that their achievements were worth making. Giving three Reith Lectures on the radio is something, but certainly not enough. Even if mounted a year or two late, the case for a Centenary Exhibition is overwhelming.

Sources for this book

"Operation Mincemeat"

The two principal sources for the main events in *Operation Mincemeat* are the book of that title, by Ben Macintyre, published 2010, and the original book *The Man Who Never Was*, by Ewan Montagu, published 1953. Most of the photos reproduced come from the National Archives, while the photo of Ronnie comes from the Reed family collection. The archives of Worcester College Oxford, through their Archivist Ms Emma Goodrum, provided details of the three weekends when members of the Security Services came to stay.

The photos and details about the Seraph Monument, come from The Citadel Archives and Museum, Charleston, South Carolina, USA, and in particular their very helpful Archives and Museum Supervisor Dwight S. Walsh Jnr.

Sources for Thomas Reed

The Certificates of Marriage and Death, as well as Thomas's prize book, are in the family collection, as are all the family photos reproduced, and the diary and letters written by Thomas and his fellow officers. I am grateful to another Folkestone resident, Hilary Tolputt, for the research she did on the parents of Thomas Reed, and the addresses where Thomas stayed as a child.

Ronnie Reed, and his early life

Ronnie's early photos of Thanet St School, his School Reports, and the early family letters, are all in the family collection. His Bing Crosby records were sold when the Dulwich house was sold in 1995. I recorded an interview with Charles Chilton, an exact contemporary of my father, in 1996, and visited him again in about 2000 and 2010. His own autobiography, with its mention of Ronnie, was broadcast as a series of programmes on BBC Radio in the 1960s. His written autobiography *Charlie's Auntie* was published by Phantom Books in August 2011 (when Charles was 94), and comes out in paperback in November. The quotation from R.V. Jones comes from his book *Most Secret War*, for which, see the later chapter on Jones. Ronnie kept a large panoramic photo of all the students and teachers at the Regent Street Polytechnic in 1929. I have given this photo to the Archives of the University of Westminster, which now holds the Polytechnic archives.

Working for the BBC, 1938-40

All the photographs and cuttings are from the family collection.

Sources for The First Double Agents

In the 1980s, my father agreed to contribute a chapter to the book *British Intelligence in the Second World War*. This was edited by Hinsley and Simkins, and was published in 1990 by Her Majesty's Stationery Office. His article became Appendix 3 of Volume 4 of the book, and was published anonymously. Its title was *Technical Problems Affecting Radio Communications by the Double-Cross Agents.* However, the second half is in effect a summary of my father's work.

The second source is a reminiscence by my father of how he was introduced to the security service, on the first day of the London blitz. This was published in the MI5 ex-servicemen's magazine Portcullis. It was kindly sent to me by a source in that organisation, who calls himself Mr Denton (not his real name, of course). The article is published here publicly for the first time.

The third source is the interview itself. What he wrote largely overlaps what he said in the interview, but as the reminiscence was carefully written down, with access to sources if needed, I have used the text, and just added extra details given in his interview.

The fourth source are four photographs of this period which my father carefully kept, three of them showing him operating a radio set in the field, and one showing a large farm building. All four are marked "Tate" in Ronnie's handwriting on the back.

Additional information has come from three books by Nigel West, commonly known as the unofficial historian of the Security Services. The first is his book "*MI5*", published in 1981. My father said he was very impressed by the detail and accuracy of the book, writing about matters which were, after all, supposed to be secret! The second is West's *Seven Spies who changed the World*, published in 1991. This has a whole chapter on Wolf Schmidt (codename Tate). As Tate was still alive at that time, West agreed to his request to conceal his real name, which was Harry Williamson, by calling him Harry Johnson. In 1993, the Faber book of Espionage was published, edited by Nigel West. West dedicated it to the memory of Harry Williamson, whose real name he now revealed, now that Williamson had died in October 1992. West also decided to "out" my father, by revealing him as the author of the Appendix published in 1990. West republished the first half of this article, but with a detailed introduction by himself with some information not recorded elsewhere. The first half of the Appendix contained general observations about wartime wireless transmission. The second half is in effect a short summary of my father's supervision of the double-agents Summer and Tate. All these sources have been pooled into what I hope is a coherent account.

Eddie Chapman: Agent Zigzag

Two books on Chapman came out in 2007: Ben Macintyre's *Agent Zigzag* was published by Bloomsbury; Nicholas Booth's *Zigzag* was published by Portrait. Macintyre's *Agent Zigzag* is so well and wittily written, that in my much shorter account, I have sometimes felt obliged to copy his wording. I hope he will regard such imitation as "the sincerest form of flattery".

Although it would be nice to think, as Ben Macintyre does, that it was Jasper Maskelyne who supervised the camouflaging of the Mosquito factory, the documents in the National Archives seem to prove it was Sir John Turner and his team. The best book on Maskelyne is *The War Magician*, by David Fisher, published by Cassells in 2004. Though subject to some adverse criticism from Richard Stokes on the internet (in particular, for not quoting sources), it does seem generally reliable. For Ronnie's visit to Lisbon, I draw on my father's memory, two days after the recorded interview, when he said he was kicking himself for not mentioning it. He also does not mention it, in his detailed report of his visit to Lisbon (in the National Archives). On his report, Tar Robertson noted, rather like a Headmaster, "This is most satisfactory." Ronnie, in his written report, said that, owing to a misunderstanding, Jarvis, our man in Lisbon, did not know Ronnie was arriving on that date, and was away at Cintra. But, said my father, the following morning they met, and Ronnie gives a detailed report on their discussions. No mention of meeting Eddie. But, of course, the whole point of sending Ronnie there was to meet Eddie and give him his instructions direct. So he must have met him. Having reported on his discussions with Jarvis in his report, Ronnie should have gone back to say what had happened the previous evening – but he forgot. Another report said that Eddie was staying on shore with a lady friend: that was presumably Anita's flat, and that should be where Ronnie met him that night.

In my main text, I omitted to mention Chapman's offer, made to my father, to assassinate Hitler (Macintyre, *Agent Zigzag*, pp. 146-8). Wiser counsels prevailed. When Heydrich was assassinated, Hitler chose to wipe out a complete village – Lidice - from the map – along with its hundreds of inhabitants. If Hitler had gone, Himmler was just as blood-thirsty.

Bletchley Park, and the army and naval code decipherments, are the subject of numerous detailed books: too many to list.

Just before this book went to press, I was shown a letter, sent after Ronnie's death, from one of his colleagues. It includes the words, "I found myself working with Ronnie soon after I joined the Office in 1947. He had already had a distinguished war: an Iron Cross used to dangle from a lamp on his desk in those early days!" So that's what happened to Eddie's Iron Cross immediately after the War.

Garbo

Nigel West's book on Garbo has now been reissued as *Operation Garbo*. Tomas Harris, Garbo's case officer, was both an artist and ran an art gallery. There is currently (Sept. 2011) a website for Tomas Harris on www.AnitaHarrisFamily.co.uk., with information constantly being added.

In the correspondence with Nigel West, my father was trying not to be mentioned at all, and refusing to comment on anything West wrote. But he also wrote the following to Mr West:

"So far as I know, the only place in which my name has been put 'in the public domain' is in your own book *MI5, 1909-1945* which I read with very considerable interest, surprise and admiration, because it was so remarkably detailed and accurate in relation to my own experience from 1940 to 1977. There was also much in it that was new to me!"

Spying for Russia

A good introduction in *World Famous Spies*, by Damon Wilson, Parragon, 1975 and 1996, pp 105-148. Much of the detail about the private lives of both the male and, in particular, the female spies, comes from a fascinating article by Natasha Walter, published in *The Guardian* for 10th May 2003. It is currently (2011) viewable on the Internet, if you Google Melinda Maclean. For detail about the Macleans generally, see *The Missing Macleans*, by Geoffrey Hoare, Viking Press, published in 1955, just before Burgess and Maclean reappeared in public, in Moscow.

I am most grateful to the current occupants of Beaconshaw, in Tatsfield, for allowing me to take several photos of the house.

I write that it was Ronnie's spotting of Jenifer Hart as a potential spy, which led to his being retained in MI5. That knowledge comes

New Zealand

The entire chapter from my memories, both direct and talking to my parents. Also documents from the time.

Ronnie at Home and Work 1960-76

The sources are almost entirely from personal memories, though the papers of the Dulwich house purchase survive.

R.V. Jones

Jones's book *Most Secret War* was first published in 1978 by Hamish Hamilton. It was reissued by Penguin in 2009. Jones later wrote a sequel to it. The first part considers intelligence in general, with some interesting thoughts about whether agents can or should ever be regarded as expendable. The second part is devoted to postscripts on *The Secret War*, and further details about the mysterious Oslo report. Entitled *Reflections on Intelligence*, it was published by Heinemann in 1989, and in paperback by Mandarin in 1990. The other lecture Jones sent to my father was entitled *1945-79, Victory into Defeat?* which was published in the Ampleforth Review, 1979, pp. 72-92.

Ronnie in Retirement

All from the author's collection of photos, and personal memories.

The "Ethics" of Spying

Dr Michael Randle kindly sent me Chapter 25 of his unpublished book on his 1991 trial. Given the great rarity of trials in which a jury deliberately ignores the instructions of the judge, this book still deserves to be published. Dr Randle also kindly commented on an earlier version of this chapter. Though my views on Blake's sentence have changed over twenty years, I still disagree with most of Dr Randle's (sadly unpublished) comments about what may be in judges' minds when sentencing, and the State's reasons for the prosecution – or pardoning – of different Russian spies. But whatever the rights and wrongs, such matters need a proper public debate.

INDEX

NOTE: A number in italic indicates an illustration